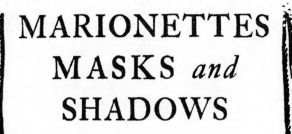

MARIONETTES MASKS *and* SHADOWS

BY
WINIFRED H. MILLS
Head of Art Department, Fairmount
Junior High Training School,
Cleveland, Ohio

&

LOUISE M. DUNN
Assistant Curator of Education,
the Cleveland Museum of
Art, Cleveland, Ohio

Illustrated
by
CORYDON BELL

Garden City, New York
DOUBLEDAY, DORAN & COMPANY, INC.
1928

This is the Tree
of the
Marionettes

To Adventurers among
Puppets and Plays

CONTENTS

Contents

ILLUSTRATIONS

HALFTONES

Marionettes

Illustrations

Illustrations

FULL PAGE LINE DRAWINGS

MARIONETTES

CHAPTER I

The Marionette—Its Family Tree

THIS is the family tree of the marionette. Its roots are deep in the life of ancient Egypt, India, Persia, China, Japan, and Java. Its great trunk springs from the soil of Greece and Rome. Its branches spread over Europe and reach to America.

Long ago, in Egypt, there were little carved figures of wood and ivory with limbs that could be made to move by the pulling of strings. We do not know for what use these little figures were intended. They may have been the very first dolls in the world or they may have been little images of the great gods which the people of that country worshiped. We do know, however, that they were treasured, and were buried with the kings and queens of ancient Egypt in their tombs near the banks of the Nile. Some people tell

I

us that the great idols in the Egyptian temples were puppets and that the priests concealing themselves inside their bodies could make them move their hands and open their mouths. This so amazed many of the people who saw them that they fell down and worshiped them.

Imagine a very long avenue with a row of carved stone figures called sphinxes on either side, leading all the way up to a great temple. Imagine a slowly moving procession of a hundred priests on its way to the temple to do honor to the great god Osiris. These priests are carrying a colossal golden boat on their shoulders. But more wonderful than the temple with its lotus-flower columns and its beautiful colors, more wonderful than the golden boat carried by these white-robed priests, was a marvelously made statue of the god Osiris, which rode in the golden boat. It moved its head constantly from side to side. The priests knew which way it wished to go by the way it turned its head. This figure of the god was a marionette. We also know that the ancient Egyptians had miniature puppet stages. One has been unearthed which has doors of ivory with the rods and wires still in their places. Among the Egyptian puppets that have been found was one of a crocodile. Its lower jaw moves on a pivot and its feet are connected with a kind of hinge.

INDIA

It is possible that India rather than Egypt may have been the first home of puppets. The people of

India believed that puppets lived with the gods long before they came down to this world. There is a story of Parvati, wife of the god Siva, that tells of a puppet which she made, that was so beautiful that she was afraid to let her husband see it, she carried it away secretly, to the Malaya Mountains. But Siva suspected his wife and followed her. When Siva saw the beauty of the puppet that she was trying to hide from him, he fell in love with it, and brought it to life.

Another story is told in India about a basket of wonderful wooden dolls that was given to a little princess. These dolls were made in such a way that when the princess touched a small wooden peg one would run and bring her a cool drink, another would fly through the air and return with a wreath of flowers, still another could dance and one could even talk. Sometimes, when puppets were made to represent the gods, they were made of pure gold and birds that could talk were placed in their mouths.

The fame of these wonderful Indian puppets reached Persia and Turkey, China and Burma, Siam and Java, in each of which countries the puppets were different and different kinds of temples and theaters were made for them. Even the elephants carved for them to ride upon were different in each country.

In many eastern countries there were two kinds of marionettes: the round kind that we know and another thin, flat kind called "Shadows." No one seems to know just when the first shadow figures were made. An old legend says they came from the time when all that the people saw of the religious ceremonies was the shadow of the priest on the walls of the sacred tent.

CHINA

We do not know just when the earliest travelers brought puppets from India to China and Japan. There is a legend that an old Chinese ruler who lived more than three thousand years ago invited a famous showman to bring his marionettes to the royal palace. This invitation delighted the showman whose name was Yen Sze. In fact, he was so anxious to please the king and his wives that he made his puppet courtiers smile at the royal ladies, which so stirred the old king's jealousy that he ordered Yen Sze's head cut off. Poor Yen Sze had to tear his puppets to pieces to make the angry old ruler believe they were not real people.

Another story of Chinese puppets is one that comes from the old city of Ping at the time it was besieged by a great warrior and his army. It happened that the king of Ping had a very crafty adviser. This adviser told the king to send for his chief marionette maker and order him to make a very large and beautiful marionette, one that could dance on the walls of the city, and this the king did. When the wives of the soldiers of the besieging army saw the beauty and grace of this marionette dancer, they became so jealous that they made their husbands give up the siege and march away at once.

It is always interesting to see how human puppets

are, no matter when or where you find them. In China, some were aristocrats and lived at Court with the Emperor and the royal family. They wore beautiful robes and gave a great deal of thought to their speech and manners. Others were very religious and lived with the priests in the temples; still others seemed to have liked the out of doors, to travel and to meet and to please the common people, and to be very much like them in all their thoughts and ways. When these plebeian marionettes traveled, they took little with them for they were poor and had few clothes and possessions. This made travel very easy. Sometimes a small box would hold the stage, properties, and all the puppets.

The master of the puppets stood inside a blue cloth sack when he gave his play. These traveling puppets were apt to be rough and ready. They loved to make the people laugh, but best of all they loved to please the children. They gave plays about every-day life, about animals that could talk, and about great Chinese heroes. They touched the hearts of the people.

PERSIA

Puppets have helped even to make friends out of enemies, as you may see in this old Persian story. One day, a puppet play was being given before the Emperor Ogotai. In this play the showman thought he would please His Majesty by showing him some of his enemies, the Chinese, being dragged along tied to the tails of horses. Instead of pleasing the Emperor, this cruelty greatly distressed him. He ordered the showman to come to his palace. When the showman came, the Emperor showed him many beautiful things that had been made by Chinese and Persian artists, explaining to the showman that both the Chinese and Persian people loved beautiful things. He endeavored to make the showman understand that if he had respect for the art of the Chinese people, he could not be their enemy.

JAPAN

From China puppets traveled to Japan where the children still hear the story of the old emperor who ordered his best showman to travel from temple to temple for he knew that the gods would be entertained by his wonderful marionette plays. Because they made their puppets entertain the gods as well as the people, may be the reason that the Japanese have become more expert in making puppets than any other people. Japanese marionettes move their hands and their fingers and can even lift their eyebrows to show scorn and surprise. The costumes for Japanese marionettes have always been of the richest silks and brocades. Special thought is given to embroidering the designs on their costumes. Sometimes their gowns are covered with jewels. When a marionette has a beautiful new gown, a boy comes forward and holds a light just in front of the marionette, so that the audience can plainly see how beautiful the costume is.

The great poets of Japan have written more than a

thousand plays for marionettes. In these plays the Japanese puppets do just the same things that Japanese people do. They have gardens and enjoy walking in them. The old ladies water the flowers, the young women play the kotes; the puppet children dance and play games, the boys fly kites, the girls carry dolls. The Japanese puppets are very silent little people. They do not talk, they simply act. There are specially trained people who read and chant their plays, and still others who are trained to play the musical instruments that accompany them.

GREECE

In the old Greek cities puppets were very much at home. They interested the older people as much as they interested the children. Puppets were taken to banquet tables and made to act. Such cities as Athens and Ephesus were rivals in the art of making them.

Greek boys and girls, instead of going to the movies, went to wonderful marionette shows. These were given in the public square, in the theaters, and even in the temples. The marionettes used in these plays could bend their heads, turn their eyes, and move their hands as though they were alive. This need not surprise us, because in those days, great engineers and mathematicians planned their mechanism. You probably remember the story of Archimedes, who burned the ships that came to attack his city of Syracuse by the use of concave mirrors. This great Archimedes, it is said, made such a wonderful marionette that it seemed to move of itself. One of the old Greek plays showed a temple in which there stood a puppet god with small figures dancing about it, and a fountain that, by means of weights and measures, jetted forth milk.

The best of the Greek puppet plays seem to have been taken from the Iliad and the Odyssey of Homer. In a play of five scenes, one scene showed the seashore, with men hammering, sawing, and building ships, a second showed the men launching their boats, a third showed the coming of a storm on the sea, the fourth showed the ships being driven toward the rocks, the last scene showed the wreck of the ships and the drowning of Ajax.

ROME

Since the Romans seem to have copied so much from the Greeks, it is not surprising that they copied the Greek marionettes. In fact, the Romans and Greeks seem to have been equally fond of them. Roman writers mentioned them in their books, Roman Emperors filled their palaces with showmen and their puppets, and built small, richly furnished theaters for them. Roman marionettes were sometimes covered with gold and silver, precious stuffs, and shining armor. Their mechanism was amazing. Almost every sort of transformation could be carried out. At one time, Roman rulers became so interested in puppets that affairs of the government were almost forgotten.

There were three kinds of Roman marionettes. The simplest kind was the Burattini, a kind of marionette that is much like a mitten. They were shown on the street corners by a showman who needed no more than two—one for each hand. It cost almost nothing to see them. The shopkeepers, gladiators, slaves, and surely the Roman children came to look whenever they heard the showman's fife. He would make them act droll little dialogues or pretend to sing popular songs. There was another kind called Fantoccini. These were jointed dolls strung on cords that were drawn across the knees of the operator. He usually sang or played some musical instrument while he made certain movements with his legs that caused the puppets to advance or retire or to move all in one direction. A third kind of marionette was manipulated by strings or wires from above.

In the tomb of the tragic Empress Marie, wife of the Emperor Honorius, who lived 365 B.C., were found the puppets of her little child. She probably cared more for these puppets than for all her jewels. The great Antiochus, when he became king of Syria, surrounded himself with mimes, burattini, and showmen, seemingly caring little for his huge empire.

When Rome fell, the gods and temples were destroyed and puppets were almost forgotten. But we find the world could not live long without them. In a very short time, when the early Christians wished to help each other to picture the precious story of the Christ, they again began to make puppets. We must now try to picture them in the great underground cities that we call catacombs—probably living in what were the world's first churches, and enacting for these persecuted peoples the scenes of the new religion. We know that these early Christians revered them, for they carved them on their tombs.

It was before the Holy Sepulcher in Jerusalem that the greatest of the early passion plays were given by marionettes, plays so simple and religious that they were greatly loved by the devout pilgrims who came to that sacred shrine. It was here that puppets were probably seen by the first crusaders who, no doubt, had much to tell of them when they returned to their far-distant homes. Puppets lived in the churches, just as they once had lived in the temples. The plays they gave were called Mysteries. These puppet mystery plays were to be seen in both the churches and the monasteries of all medieval Europe. They were solemn festivals of sacred commemoration. Into the naves and chapels of these early churches, large wooden stages were built, carpets were spread on the floors, tapestries were hung on the walls. At the back of these stages, evergreen trees were placed and in front of the trees there were stones. These were covered with plants and moss in imitation of the hills and valleys and pathways of the Holy Land. Everything was so arranged that these marionettes could give the most dramatic scenes in the life of Christ. The little figures were carved from wood, colored to life, richly clothed, adapted by mechanisms so that their limbs could be made to move by the action of springs and levers.

As time went on the people seemed to lose much of

their strong religious fervor. Marionettes did the same. Finally almost ceasing to be religious they became interested only in entertaining people. At last Savonarola banished them from the churches of Florence, and in the year 1550 the Council of Trent tried to banish all marionettes from the churches. The Council did this because it felt that marionettes were very irreligious.

Then the puppets rebelled and forsook the church for the theater. Thereupon they were accused of witchcraft and magic, were tortured, burned, beheaded, and even buried alive. All this was done in the XVIth Century. But all these indignities did not drive the marionettes far from the churches. They established themselves just outside the church grounds. Here they were sure to be on the days when crowds of people were coming to the great church celebrations. The plays they gave were episodes taken from the Holy Scriptures. These episodes taken from the miracles came to be known as Miracle Plays, and these plays became even more popular than the Mystery Plays that had been given inside the churches.

Sometimes puppets received invitations to visit great knights and ladies in their castles. They were eager for such invitations because they enjoyed the experiences of traveling. As always happens in travel, they saw new things to interest them and met new people, many of whom were quite different from their earlier and more serious-minded friends. They enjoyed the life of the castle, the songs of the wandering minstrels, and the heroic stories that the traveling bards told in the evenings about the fire in the great halls. They liked the noble lords and ladies, their speech and manners' and dress. These marionettes became what you might call aristocrats.

The marionettes that were religious found a home in the quiet of the monasteries. They were the marionettes that were scholarly and were interested in Latin plays as well as in the Mysteries and Sacred Dramas.

The greater number of marionettes preferred to live in the towns with the common people and to know what was going on. These puppets were full of health and good humor. It was this sort of marionette who changed his name and his character almost everywhere he went. If he were in Naples, he was Scaramuccia; in Venice, he was Messer Pantaleone; in Bergamo, he was Arlequino; in France, he was Guignol or Polichinello; in Germany, he was Hans Wurst and Kaspare; in Holland, he was Jean Pickel Herring; and in England, he was Mr. Punch.

ITALY

In Italy at about this time every kind of marionette was very popular. Especially popular were the Burattini. These little figures consisted of a head and two hands held together by a large cloak within which was hidden the hand of the manipulator, who made the puppet act by the movements of his fingers and wrist. The curious word, Burattini, possibly came from a kind of coarse, durable cloth of bright colors known as Burato, which was used for clothing this type of puppet. One of these Burattini was called Arleechino. He was a great baby and played the part of a servant. His dress was made from triangles of red, blue, yellow, and violet pieces of Burato cloth. He wore a small hat that scarcely covered his head. His little shoes had no soles. Michael Angelo, it is said, did not like his head and face. He remodeled them to suit the Burattini's character, which was an odd mixture of ignorance, ingenuity, stupidity, and grace. Listen to his speech: "Kind sir, I know that you are in want of a servant, after having made 327 changes in a year, and I hope to make up the round number. I am a man who knows how to do everything—eating, drinking, sleeping, and making love to the maids. The only fault I have is that I do not like work. I shall be as punctual as an idler, as faithful as a domestic thief, as secret as an earthquake, and as watchful as a cat. As to my honesty, surely no man can call me a thief, but rather a clever mathematician who finds things before their masters lose them."

You may like to know how marionettes came by their name. One day, in the year 944, in the city of Venice, twelve beautiful maidens went forth from their homes to marry twelve young men at the church of Santa Maria della Salute. Suddenly a band of Barbary pirates landed near the church, attacked the crowd, and in the confusion that arose, carried away the maidens. In a short time the young men of Venice recovered from the shock, jumped into their ships, followed and overtook the pirates. After much fighting, they rescued the brides. From that very day it was the custom in Venice to celebrate the anniversary of this event by a great festival. Always on the last day of the festival came the marriage of twelve beautiful young women to twelve handsome young men. The wedding gowns and doweries were provided by the state from the public treasury. In the course of time, this led to so much jealousy and so many quarrels among the young men and women of Venice, that the city decided to substitute life-sized wooden dolls for the maidens. By and by, the Venetian toy makers began to make little figures that were exactly like the large figures, to sell as toys for the children. These were called "little maries" or "marionettes."

When one learns to know the people of Italy, he can easily understand how puppets might feel more at home there than in any other country in the world. The Italian people love music and color and motion and life, above all else they love heroes, their great adventures and romances. All these things are equally dear to the hearts of the marionettes. They repay the sympathy of the Italian people by keeping alive for them their great heroes and hero tales. The people might have forgotten many of their great stories had it not been for the puppets. The legend of the Court of Charlemagne, the story of golden-haired Roland, which Tailhfer sang before William of Normandy at the Battle of Hastings, have been acted by puppets in Italy for more than three hundred years. One may still see all the characters that were in the story as it was told in the Xth Century. There is

Rinaldo of Montauban, his horse Bayard, his sword Flamberge, Malagigi, the magician, and Ganelon, the traitor, fair Clarissa and Charlemagne himself. Italian boys and girls learn much of their history from puppets. Sometimes it requires a whole year to give one of their great plays like *Orlando Furioso* or the story of the seven Paladins. From Italy marionettes traveled to all the other countries of Europe, to France, Spain, Germany, and England. Finally they came to the United States.

FRANCE

You may wish to know how puppets found their way from Italy to France. There were two brothers, Giovanni and Francesco Briocchi. Francesco was a skilful wood carver and mechanic. Giovanni was very clever with his speeches and jokes. As children, they loved marionettes. They hardly knew which they enjoyed more, sitting in the audience watching the play, or standing behind the stage watching their friends manipulate the puppets. They decided that when they grew up they would be puppeteers, make their own puppets and travel from town to town and to the fair land of which they had heard so many interesting tales. This they did. Giovanni made the figures skilfully and dressed them beautifully. Francesco made them say and do such clever and amusing things that their fame went before them into small towns and into the large cities. When they had made enough money they said, "Now we can go to France. We can easily carry our little stage and puppets on

our backs. We can earn our way by giving plays."
This they did, to the delight of all who saw them.
Finally they reached the city of Paris. In those days
great fairs were held where people came to buy and
sell and to make merry. Here was just the place for
Giovanni and Francesco. When the fairs became
permanent the brothers decided to settle down and
make a real home for their marionettes. This at first
was a simple kind of theater, but later came to have
every beautiful thing that French taste and ingenuity
could provide. One day the king and queen made them
a visit and engaged them to come out to their
beautiful château at St. Germain en Laye and give
puppet plays for their young son, the dauphin, and
his friends. In the records of France you may still
see the account as it stands: "Sept. 1669, to Jean
Briocchi, divertir les enfants de France, 1365 livres."
When the Frenchmen saw the success of the Italian
showmen, they, too, began to make puppets and to
take them to the places where people gathered who
might be willing to spend a few sous for entertainment. Among these was an old dentist, who found it
difficult to earn a living. He made some marionettes
and a clever little boxlike stage with a curtain about
it. It was just large enough for him to stand inside
and manipulate the puppets. He decided to take his
stand to the Pont Neuf, one of the principal bridges
of Paris. Here he would pull teeth when anyone
needed his services and for the rest of the time would
entertain the people. He had also a very celebrated
monkey, called Fagotin, that he knew would attract

a crowd. Fagotin he dressed as a sentry, gave him a sword, and trained him to march up and down in front of the little puppet booth. One day a great poet, whose name was Cyrano de Bergerac, was crossing the bridge and stopped, as did most of the people, to see Fagotin and the puppets. It happened that the poet had a very large nose and was a very sensitive person. When he saw Fagotin marching up and down and making grimaces, he thought he must surely be making fun of his large nose. At this, the poet was so angry that he challenged him to a duel. Poor little Fagotin drew his sword with the air of a master of the foils, only to be slain by the irate poet.

The French people, like the Italians, had a great many heroes celebrated in song and romance. It certainly would have been poor taste on the part of the Italian puppets to have overlooked this. In a short time the puppets forgot Italy and were at home in many new rôles of French literature. New plays were written for them. When that great struggle, the French Revolution, came, the puppets took sides. Some were on the side of the poor starving people, others were unwilling to give up their lives of ease and luxury. During the Reign of Terror many puppets were beheaded. In fact, while one group of people was beheading King Louis XVI and his queen, Marie Antoinette, another group in almost the same place was beheading poor Punchinello. Many puppets, however, survived, and a whole book might be written about the history of puppets in France and the great men and women who have loved them.

SPAIN

In Spain, the puppets first appeared in the churches, presenting great scenes from the Bible. At first their garments were simple and beautiful, but later they were so bejeweled and vulgar that they offended the good taste of the people and the puppets were driven out. Spain is the only country in which a marionette was ever made a citizen and baptized. Don Quixote saw them, and the great Emperor Charles V, in his retirement in the monastery of Cremona, spent many days with the famous scholar, Torriani, making puppet soldiers and bull fighters, with such skill that they were really able to fight.

ENGLAND

As in almost all other countries, the earliest English puppets were those which gave religious plays in the churches. From the churches, they went out among the people, still giving plays founded on the Bible stories and the lives of the saints. These plays were combinations of shadowgraph and marionette, and the English people sometimes called them "motions." English puppets were also very fond of going to the fairs. Here is the pamphlet of a play given at the Fair of St. Bartholomew in 1641:"Here a knave in a fool's coat, with a trumpet sounding or a drum beating, invites you to see his puppets. Here a rogue, like a wild woodman, or in antic shape like

Marionette play, "Men of Iron," given by ninth year pupils,
Fairmount Junior High School, Cleveland, Ohio

an incubus, desires your company to see his motion."

Probably the most popular puppet play in England in those days was one called "The Old Creation of the world, with the addition of Noah's Flood." The best scene showed "Noah and his family coming out of the ark with all the animals, two by two, and all the fowls of the air seen in prospect sitting upon trees; likewise, over the ark is the sun rising in a glorious manner, moreover, a multitude of angels in a double rank, the angels ringing bells. Likewise, machines descending from above, double, with Dives rising out of hell and Lazarus seen in Abraham's bosom; besides several dancing gigs, sarabands and country dances, with merry conceits of Squire Punch and Sir John Spendall."

This play was given for fifty-two successive nights. Mr. Powell, the clever but roguish fellow who owned these puppets, once set up his little theater just outside the colonnades of Covent Garden, opposite the parish church of St. Paul. He began his plays at the sound of the church bells, and was successful in diverting so many from the church services that he was severely reproved by the churchmen. It was this same clever Powell, who had a very famous puppet called Lady Jane, who went to Paris every month and came back with a trunk full of gowns of the latest fashion. These marionette style shows delighted all the ladies of fashion in London, including the queen.

About 1642, all regular theaters were abolished in England, but marionette theaters were not included. You can scarcely imagine the good fortune this meant for them, for they inherited everything that had belonged to the great theaters, all the music and opera, the dramas, the tragedies, and the comedies. When news of this reached Italy and France, many showmen started at once for England. They knew they could gather pennies on the way from almost every pocket. The regular price of these puppet plays was but two pence, but a fine play like *The Gun Powder Plot* cost eighteen pence. There were plays about giants and fairies, about Robin Hood and Little John, about St. George and the dragon, and a hundred other tales.

All the great writers of those days now began to write plays for marionettes. Beautiful new theaters were built for them. It became the fashion to go to puppet plays. Ben Jonson says that many great ladies went every day.

In 1688, Punchinello changed his name to Mr. Punch and he married Judy. When they had a son and went to housekeeping, then the quarrels began. You may have had the pleasure of hearing some of them. Punch had a wide circle of friends and some of them were interested in politics. Many great Englishmen, like Addison, Steele, Fielding, Milton, and Byron, were glad to tell him what to say that would help to set the people thinking. Some of the English puppets disliked cities and were only happy when they were going up and down the lovely English roads, traveling among the villages and country people. There you can still find them.

To-day the most beautiful English puppets are being made by Mr. William Simmonds who began his work with puppet plays for village children. Mr. Simmonds manipulates his own puppets as he cleverly improvises songs, dances, and pantomimes.

GERMANY—AUSTRIA—RUSSIA

Before we follow marionettes to our own country, we ought to take a little time to see them in Germany, Austria, and Russia. These peoples were skilful in wood carving and made their puppets beautifully. Marionettes were used in the early churches of these countries, and gave Holy Plays before the high altars. Then they went to the castles and at last to the theaters. It was only in Germany that great musicians wrote music for them. In 1762, Haydn wrote for them his toy symphony, "The Children's Fair," which was followed by five operettas given in the theater at Eisenstadt. Probably the great *Passion Play* at Oberammergau has grown out of the early puppet plays that were given in the monasteries and cathedrals.

The city of Munich built a little theater for Papa Schmidt, an old man who had spent all his life giving puppet plays. This was done through citizens who felt indebted to him for the pleasure he had given them as children. They said, the least they could do was to build him a theater, a place for himself and his daughter and their thousand puppets, that included all the characters in the beautiful fairy tales.

In Vienna, the artist Richard Teschner has created

some remarkable modern marionettes. He has carved them most delicately from wood and has shown great ingenuity in the way he has put his little figures together.

In Bohemia, the puppets were interested in politics, if they were serious, and in comedies if they were not serious. In Hungary, they traveled with the gypsies. In Poland and Russia, they are loved by all the common people, and at Christmas celebrations still appear in their ancient rôles as Joseph and Mary and the Christ Child, as wise men, shepherds, and angels.

AMERICA

Puppets are not new in America. The North American Indians for hundreds of years used them in their great ceremonies. The Hopi Indians used marionettes to represent the mystic maidens who in ancient times gave them, according to their legends, the corn and other seeds. This ceremony is performed in a darkened room—in the center of which is a wooden framework. The marionettes are placed on a stage or platform and when the corn maiden's song begins, the figures bend their bodies forward and backward in time to the music as they grind the meal between the miniature grindstones before them. The little figures are so cleverly manipulated that they even rub their faces with meal as the young Indian girls are accustomed to do. During the ceremony, two symbolic marionette birds are made to walk back and forth, on the framework, above the maidens, seeming to utter bird calls. The Hopi Indians also made marionettes of their enemies, the serpents, which represented floods and misfortune.

Most of the marionettes that we have known in America, until a few years ago, were Italian. They were very shy and would not leave their Italian neighborhoods. They often spoke no English. They gave plays about heroes that we know little or nothing about.

In America, there is a growing list of friends of the marionette. Probably the name best known to you will be that of Tony Sarg, a charming artist who has taken his puppet plays to the largest cities in our country and delighted us with his *Rip Van Winkle, Rose and the King,* and *Don Quixote.* The manager of his marionettes, Mr. Matthew Searle, is also an artist of ingenuity and taste.

In Chicago, the splendid work of Mr. and Mrs. Maurice Brown made new friends for the marionette. Mr. Perry Dilley introduced marionettes and guignol to the people of California. He produced a great number of interesting plays and all of his puppets are exceptionally fine. Mr. William Duncan and Mr. Edward Mabley, creators of the "Tatterman Marionettes," have brought to the marionette stage unusual imagination and skill, which is admirably shown in their *The Melon Thief, The King of the Golden River,* and *Pierre Patelin.*

Madge Anderson has written beautifully of her puppet heroes. Mrs. Helen Haiman Joseph has written an excellent *Book of Marionettes.* If it were possible one would like to add the complete list of all those who are carrying on the great tradition of the marionette. The interest, already created, leads one to hope that America may take her place high up in the marion-ette tree.

CHAPTER II

The Marionette—Its Famous Friends

EVERY person is proud of his famous friends. If we know a great artist, engineer, or traveler, we think we are fortunate. Can you imagine having so many famous friends that you could not count them? This has been the good fortune of marionettes. The names of all their Egyptian friends seem to be lost. But it is not so with their Grecian friends. Archimedes, Socrates, and Plato are the names of three famous friends that have come down to us. Archimedes, the greatest inventor of his time, liked puppets, it is said, because he could devise so many clever ways of making them move and appear human. Socrates probably cared nothing for the mechanism. He enjoyed taking a puppet in his own hands, asking it clever questions, and then furnishing the equally clever answers. These most unusual conversations would soon gather about him a crowd of Athenian men and women, who were greatly interested in his humor, irony, and whimsical paradoxes. The dialogues would probably go on and on until his scolding wife, Xantippe, appeared. Plato also cared little for their mechanism, but like his great master, Socrates, was interested only when they were made to talk about the very serious things of life, or when he saw them representing the gods and heroes in the beautiful scenes of the plays given on the small stages built for them in one part of the great theaters.

Kings and queens were among the famous Roman friends of puppets. You may remember that puppets were found in the tomb of the Empress Marie and that the Emperor Antiochus cared so much for them that he neglected the affairs of his great empire. He had clever puppet makers as part of his royal household, and delighted in planning the plays they were to give. He designed the stage settings, and he sometimes assisted the royal puppeteers.

In India, China, and Japan, the great rulers were greatly interested in puppets, and required their presence at court.

One of the most interesting stories of a royal friend of the marionettes is that of the Emperor Charles V of Spain. This strange ruler's reason was clouded. His devoted minister tried in many ways to divert his beloved king, and finally succeeded when he found that the king could be interested in puppets. Puppet soldiers, puppet generals, puppet kings caught his imagination. The cleverest hands of Spain made them, by the hundred, for His Majesty, who handled them with such interest and pleasure that his reason was finally restored. Two other great kings could be added to the list of royal friends—they are Saladin and Louis XIV of France.

There is a long list of famous literary friends. Greatest of these is Shakespeare, who not only enjoyed marionettes, but wrote plays for them. Many people are surprised when they learn that *Midsummer Night's Dream* and *Julius Cæsar* were written for marionettes. Shakespeare's friend, Ben Jonson, wrote a marionette play, *Every Man in His Humor*. Another great literary friend was Cervantes. Some day you may wish to take his story of Don Quixote and turn some of its wonderful scenes into a play for marionettes. If you do so, you may be sure that their immortal author would approve of your venture.

In France, among their many friends, was the great dramatist Voltaire. At first he disliked marionettes thoroughly. For it happened that they had made fun of him, and, naturally, that was more than this great wit could stand. Finally, the story goes, he was invited to visit a friend who had a little marionette theater and some puppets. When Voltaire took the strings in his own hands, his feeling for them changed. He found they could be made to say witty things, and to make fun of one's enemies. It ended by his writing short plays for them to act.

George Sand, the famous French novelist, made a very simple but delightful puppet theater for her little boy, Maurice, and set the fashion for puppets among her literary friends. Stories could be told of many other famous French friends, of Molière, Fontaine, Doré, and Rousseau. Great French writers still love marionettes. You probably know two of these: Maurice Maeterlinck. and Anatole France.

When we go to Italy, we find other friends, but none greater than Michael Angelo. Picture this artist modeling heads for marionettes. We wonder what they looked like and what became of them. His great patron, Lorenzo de Medici, had a puppet theater built for his palace in Florence.

Marionettes have had famous musicians as their friends. If you are interested in music, you will enjoy reading about Joseph Haydn and the five toy symphonies that he wrote for marionettes.

Goldoni, the greatest Italian writer of comedies, was born in Venice, that city in which, you remember, puppets were first called marionettes. He lived near the street where most of the puppet makers lived and had their shops. As a child he played puppet games with many other children in a little park near his home. When he was seven years old he wrote a puppet play and invited his friends to come to see and hear it. He enjoyed writing plays that made them laugh. When Goldoni grew up he was still the friend of puppets because he felt that they had helped him in learning the art of play writing.

The German poet, Goethe, was a friend of puppets from his childhood. When he was about the age of seven, a friend of his good mother made some puppets and sent them to him and his sister for a Christmas present. The mother had a happy thought. She made a little stage and set it in the doorway of a room, just off the living room. On Christmas morning, after the children had seen their presents, she had the family sit down before the closed door. When she opened it, there was a kind of porch concealed with a mysterious curtain. The children were curious and eager to know what was behind that half-transparent veil. The mother, however, bade each sit down upon his stool. At length, Goethe says, "All were silent, a whistle gave the signal, the curtain rolled aloft and showed us the interior of a temple painted in deep red colors. The high priest, Samuel, appeared with Jonathan, and their strange alternating voices seemed to me the most striking thing on earth. Shortly after entered Saul, overwhelmed with confusion at the impatience of that heavy-limbed warrior who had defied him and all his people. But how glad was I when the dapper son of Jesse, with his crook and shepherd's pouch and sling, came hopping forth and said, 'Dread king and sovereign lord, let no one's heart sink down because of this. If your majesty will grant me leave, I will go out to battle with this blustering giant!'

"Here ended the first act, leaving the spectators more curious than ever to see what further would happen—each praying that the music might soon be done. At last the curtain rose again. David devoted the flesh of the monsters to the fowls of the air and the beasts of the field; the Philistine scorned and bullied him, stamped mightily with both his feet, and at length fell like a mass of clay, affording a splendid

termination to the piece, and then the virgins sang a
song: 'Saul hath slain his thousands, but David his
ten thousands.' The giant's head was borne before his
little victor, who received the king's beautiful daughter to wife.'' This is part of the description that Goethe
wrote when he grew up and became a famous man.

Do read the delightful and vivid description which
Constantin Stanislavsky gives of his boyish experiences with marionettes in his autobiography, *My
Life in Art*. "We had decided to exchange the living
actors for actors made of pasteboard and to begin the
construction of a marionette theater with scenery,
effects, and a full line of theatrical necessities. The
marionette theater demanded expenditures. We
needed a large table to put in the large doorway.
While above and beneath it, that is above and beneath the marionette stage, the openings were covered with sheets. In this manner, the public sat in one
room, the auditorium and the other room, which was
united to the first, was the stage and all its accessories. It was there that we worked, we the artists, the
designers, the stage managers, and the inventors of
all sorts of scenic effects. My oldest brother also
joined us. He was an excellent draftsman, and a fine
inventor of stage effects. His help was important because he had a little money, and we needed capital
for our work.

"We began to paint scenery. At first we painted
on wrapping paper which tore and crumpled, but we
did not lose heart for we thought that with time, as
soon as we became rich (for we were to charge ten

kopeks as admission), we would buy pasteboard and glue the painted wrapping paper to it. From the moment that we began to feel ourselves managers and directors of the new theater, that was being built according to our plans, our lives became full. There was something to think about every minute. There was a great deal to do. In the drawer of the table there always lay hidden some piece of theatrical work, the figure of a marionette which was to be painted and dressed, a piece of scenery, a bush, a tree, or the plan and sketches for a new production. In the margins of my books and copy books there were always sketches of scenery or a geometric drawing. We always chose moments of catastrophic character. For instance, an act from *The Corsair*, which called for a sea quiet in the daylight but stormy all night with a wrecked ship, with heroes swimming for their lives, with the appearance of a lighthouse, an escape from a watery grave, the rising of the moon, prayer, and dawn.

"These performances were always sold out, notwithstanding the high price of admission. Many people came to see them, some to encourage us, others to amuse themselves. Our promenades between lessons took on a very deep meaning. Before that we went to the Kugnetsky Bridge to buy the photographs of circus artists. But with the appearance of our theater, there appeared a need for all sorts of material for scenery and marionettes. Now we were no longer too lazy to take a walk. We bought all sorts of pictures, books with landscapes and costumes which served as material for the scenery and the dramatic personæ of our theater. These were the first volume of a rapidly increasing library."

Perhaps that friend who has done most to keep the world still interested in marionettes is Gordon Craig. He is a great English artist who sees them not as so much wood and cloth pulled about by a few strings at the whim of careless people, but rather as real creatures, human or more than human, quiet and dignified, as the gods of old. It has been his delight to give them again the great rôles of literature. He, too, invited the greatest actors of Europe to come and learn from them.

Possibly you are asking what it is that gives such friendships to the marionette. Perhaps none of its great friends could answer. The marionette is quiet, submissive, dignified, and mysterious. It becomes a different thing in every hand. It expresses every mood, thought, and fancy of the one who pulls the strings. What will it do in your hands?

CHAPTER III

Choosing Your Play

IT MAY not always be easy to find just the play you wish for your marionettes. If you should go to your library and ask for a marionette play, it is possible that the librarian would have very little to offer you. But if you should go to her and ask for a good story that you could make into a marionette play, you would probably be surprised to see how many books she would place before you. You might even feel confused when you came to make your choice. Suppose that you wish to give a humorous play. Begin by making a list of the very best of the humorous books:

Alice in Wonderland—Carroll
Alice, Through the Looking Glass—Carroll
Gulliver's Travels—Swift
Pinocchio, The Story of a Marionette—Lorenzini
Don Quixote—Cervantes
Midsummer Night's Dream—Shakespeare
Peter and Wendy—Barrie
Rip Van Winkle—Irving
Just-So Stories—Kipling
Arabian Nights—Edited by Colum
Uncle Remus—Harris

Marionettes—Masks and Shadows

Rose and the Ring—Thackeray
Tom Sawyer—Clemens
Wind in the Willows—Grahame
Tales of Laughter—Wiggin and Smith

You will find that it is not at all difficult to turn the vivid and amusing characters of these books into marionettes. Neither is it difficult to turn these stories into marionette plays.

First: Make a list of the most important incidents in the story.

Second: Decide upon the number of scenes that you think necessary for your play.

Third: Decide upon the number of characters required for these scenes.

These three things you must do if your play is to be only the simplest kind of a Burattini play, if it is to be a shadow play, or a marionette play.

If you are not experienced in making marionette plays, you may think that you need a great many characters to act your story. But the more you learn about marionette plays, the more you will be surprised to find how few characters, and incidents, and scenes you will need. Choose only those which are most important. This means that you should know your story very well indeed before you begin to make your play. When you thoroughly know your story and all the characters in it, all that they say and do, you will enjoy your play-making quite as much as your play-giving.

Let us choose one or two humorous books and see how we can turn them into a marionette play. We

Scenes from the marionette play, "*Adventures of Alice*,"
given by ninth year pupils of Fairmount Junior High School
at the Cleveland Museum of Art. Marionettes made by

might choose *Alice in Wonderland* and *Through the Looking Glass*. You remember how the story of *Alice in Wonderland* begins? Alice falls asleep under the tree and the white rabbit passes by. So one might select:

Incident   I. Alice and the White Rabbit
Incident   II. Alice and the Caterpillar
Incident III. Alice and Tweedle Dum and Tweedle Dee
Incident IV. Alice and Humpty Dumpty
Incident   V. Alice and the Duchess, the Cheshire Cat, the Cook and the Pig Baby
Incident VI. Alice and the Hatter, the March Hare and the Dormouse

Of course, a dozen plays could be made from these two books, but these six incidents will be quite enough for your purpose. A good play, as you know, must not be too long, it must begin in the right way, the story must hold together, and it must be very interesting all the time, and it must have the right ending. The above six incidents were selected with these requirements in mind.

Now, how many acts shall we have? Since this is a dream story, the play might begin by showing Alice falling asleep under the trees, and the White Rabbit running past, and then Alice jumping up and following him. This part of the play we might call a Prologue since it begins the story. Then follow with:

Act   I. Scene: In the woods
Act II. Scene: In the Duchess's kitchen
Act III. Scene: The mad tea party

To bring the play to an end, there might be a closing scene, or epilogue, showing Alice waking from her dream and becoming herself again.

We must now decide just how many characters are really necessary in these six incidents. Let us take a pencil and make the list as we find them in these three acts:

Prologue: Alice and the White Rabbit.
  Act   I. Alice, the Caterpillar, Tweedle Dee, Tweedle Dum, Humpty Dumpty
  Act II. Alice, the Duchess, the Pig Baby, the Cook, the Cheshire Cat
  Act III. Alice, the Hatter, the March Hare, the Dormouse
Epilogue. Alice and the White Rabbit

Here we have made from six important incidents, in the two stories about Alice, a marionette play of three acts, with a cast of thirteen characters. This play might be called *The Adventures of Alice*.

Possibly you and your friends are much interested in heroes and heroines and would prefer a hero play made from such stories as:

The Book of King Arthur and His Noble Knights—MacLeod
Sohrab and Rustum—Arnold
The Boys' Iliad—Perry
The Boys' Odyssey—Perry
Adventures of Ulysses—Lamb
Adventures of Odysseus and the Tale of Troy—Colum
Robin Hood—Pyle
The Tales of Troy and Greece—Lang
Stories of Charlemagne—Church
The Story of Roland—Baldwin
Seven Champions of Christendom—Johnson

Beowulf—Cartwright
Sigurd, the Volsung—Morris
Joan of Arc—Boutet de Monvel
Ivanhoe—Scott
Daniel Boone—White
Norse Stories Retold—Mabie
The Cid—Wilson
Britain Long Ago—Wilmot-Buxton

Instead of hero plays you may be interested in plays of adventure. The list of excellent books of adventure is a long one, as you know. Here are just a few that are waiting to be turned into wonderful marionette plays:

Robinson Crusoe—Defoe
Boy's Froissart—Lanier
The Wonder Book—Hawthorne
The Boys Percy—Lanier
Otto of the Silver Hand—Pyle
Black Arrow—Stevenson
Tales from the Alhambra—Irving
William Tell—Schiller
Treasure Island—Stevenson
Men of Iron—Pyle
The Story of the Canterbury Pilgrims—Darton
The Lance of Kanana—French
The Book of Bravery—Lanier
The Last of the Mohicans—Cooper
With Spurs of Gold—Greene
The Golden Perch—Hutchinson
Captains Courageous—Kipling

Let us take one of these, Howard Pyle's *Men of Iron*, a story laid in England in the time of King Henry IV. The list of important incidents is a long one.

1. Myles parting from the old servant.
2. Myles presenting his father's letter to the Earl of Mackworth.
3. Myles meeting with Gascoyne.
4. Myles meeting with Sir James Lee.
5. Myles at play with the boys.
6. The ball flies over into the ladies' garden.
7. Myles and Lady Alice in the garden.
8. Myles, discovered by the Earl of Mackworth, learns that the Earl is befriending him.
9. Arrival of King Henry at Devlen Castle.
10. The knighting of Myles.
11. Myles' challenge to the Earl of Alban, his father's deadly enemy.
12. The combat between the Earl of Alban and Myles.
13. The triumph of Myles and his request for the hand of Lady Alice.

When you have studied the story of *Men of Iron* and made your list of important incidents, you will find that four acts are sufficient for your play:

Act   I. Courtyard of Devlen Castle
Act II. The ladies' garden
Act III. The great hall in Devlen Castle
Act IV. The tournament ground and the royal pavilions and gallery.

The list of characters is long but it gives an opportunity to many boys and girls in a class to make marionettes and to have a part in the play. Here is the list of characters:

1. Myles as a boy in Acts I and II
2. Myles as a man in Acts III and IV
3. The old Servant
4. The Armorer
5. The Bear Trainer
6. The Bear
7. Gascoyne
8. Walter Blunt
9. The Squire
10. Sir James Lee

11. Earl of Mackworth
12. The Pryor
13. The Earl of Alban
14. The Minstrel
15. The Jester
16. Lady Alice
17. Lady Anne
18. Black Horse
19. Gray Horse
20. The Pigeons

Marionette plays are exactly like all other plays. They need songs and dances, and many things that will be certain to interest the audience. Here is a list of the incidents that were added to this play when it was given by the boys and girls of Fairmount Junior High School in Cleveland, Ohio:

1. An Italian bear trainer, who whistled a jolly tune while his bear danced and did his tricks.
2. The song of the Armorer as he worked at his forge. (The forge was so made and wired that every stroke of the hammer on the anvil gave forth a shower of sparks.)
3. A fight between Myles and the young squire, Walter Blunt.
4. Practice at the pells to show the training of the squires of that day.
5. Lady Alice's little dance.
6. Lady Anne's song as she plays her lute.
7. Alice's tame pigeon that flew down to her shoulder.
8. The wandering minstrel with his lute and his ballad of Chevy Chase.
9. The antics, capers, and songs of the jester.

In order to prepare the audience for the play and to carry every person back in imagination to the time of this play, an announcer was chosen, who, in the costume of that day, came before the curtain and gave the introduction to the play. This announcer was chosen with great care because his part was so important. He was responsible for carrying his audience back into the days of chivalry, not only by his speech

and costume, but by his tone of voice and his gestures.
Here is the prologue that one of the children wrote:

Hark ye! Hark ye! Ye who came to see
Enacted here some scenes of chivalry.

The castle gate swings wide its door
Scenes long since gone return to us once more.

Into times dim and far we bid you gaze,
Down the long vista to the tournament days.

Towers and turrets and battlements old,
Squires and pages and bachelors bold.

Lords and ladies step out from past ages
While knights and earls throw down their iron gages.

Then men were bold and strongly said their say
And there were few who dared to say them "nay."

The minstrel, too, did tune on lyre his hero's deeds
And sang of love, of hope, and needs.

Bears oft came dancing in court and in hall,
Trained by their master to heed beck and call.

Fair maids in latticed bowers were seen dancing,
Fantastic and gay, a jester comes prancing.

Hark! a blare of trumpets sounds as in a dream
And lo! the king and train in mail and helmets gleam.

Mid fluttering scarfs, the Queen of Beauty sat
While in the lists brave knights did wage combat.

All these have you from history's page
Now shall you see them pictured on our stage.

Grant us your patience, lend eyes and ears as well,
The truth our puppets now will strive to tell.

There were many things in this play that every member of the class was uncertain about. No one knew about the kinds of costumes that were worn in England in the time of Henry IV. Neither did anyone know about houses, gardens, and furniture, nor about the armor and the musical instruments of that day until he had studied reference books. Here is a list of some of the books that were found helpful:

Heraldry—*Complete Guide to Heraldry*—Fox-Davies
Furniture—*How to Know Period Styles in Furniture*—Kimberly
Tapestry—*Bayeux Tapestry*—Belloc
Tapestry—*Bayeux Tapestry*—Bruce
Tapestry—*The Practical Book of Tapestry*—Hunter
Weapons—*Armour and Weapons*—Foulkes
Customs and Life of the Time—*History of Everyday Things in England*—Quennell
Songs and Ballads—*Songs of England*—Hatton
Costumes—*The Heritage of Dress*—Webb
Costumes—*British Costumes During Nineteen Centuries*—Ashdown

The Museum of Art and the Historical Museum can be visited for first-hand information. Librarians, history, art, and English teachers can be counted upon for help. The librarian will help you to find the kind of book you wish, and will be glad to help find reference books and pictures. The history teacher will help you in learning about the life and customs of the people who are of the time of your play. The English teacher can be of invaluable help to you in working out the development of your play. Last, but not least, you will have very great need of your art and manual training teachers. They will help you in learning how to make your marionettes, how to make your marionette stage, how to make your scenery and properties, how to light the stage, what colors to use in your costumes and in your scenery, and how to place both your scenery and your actors on the stage. They will also assist you in planning the stage pictures.

Moreover, you may be interested in other literary plays made from such stories as:

Birds' Christmas Carol—Wiggin
Little Women—Alcott
Prince and the Pauper—Clemens
Oliver Twist—Dickens
Cricket on the Hearth—Dickens
The Tempest—Shakespeare
The Merchant of Venice—Shakespeare
Heidi—Spyri
Master Skylark—Bennett
Gabriel and the Hour Book—Stein
Rip Van Winkle—Irving
David Copperfield—Dickens
The Christmas Carol—Dickens
The King of the Golden River—Ruskin

Should you like the story of *The Childhood of David Copperfield*, some such interesting incidents as the following might be chosen:

1. David and Peggotty.
3. David meets Captain Peggotty, Emily, and Mrs. Gummidge.
3. David and Emily.
4. David in the schoolroom.
5. Betsy Trotwood and Master Dick.
6. David and Betsy Trotwood.

The characters in these incidents are:

1. David
2. Peggotty
3. Captain Peggotty
4. Mrs. Gummidge
5. Emily
6. Ham

7. Tommy Traddles
8. Schoolboy
9. Mr. Schoolmaster
10. Mr. Schoolmaster's assistant
11. Betsy Trotwood
12. Master Dick

13. The mouse

Five acts would give the story:

Act   I. The Copperfield sitting room
Act II. Inside the boathouse
Act III. Along the seashore
Act IV. In the schoolroom
Act   V. Betsy Trotwood's garden

Since every act of a play should help in telling the story, in solving the principal problem, and in bringing about the proper ending, this arrangement might be made:

Act   I. David reads and talks to Peggotty about her brother's boathouse. Peggotty invites David to spend a week there.
Act II. In the boathouse. David meets Peggotty's family.
Act III. By the seashore. David plays with Emily, who sings a song, and David tells Emily how much he will miss her when he goes away to school.
Act IV. In the schoolroom. The cruel schoolmaster and his assistant. David decides to run away.
Act   V. Betsy Trotwood's garden. David finds a home with his good Aunt Betsy and gentle old Master Dick.

At the same time that Charles Dickens was writing *David Copperfield* and other stories about the people he knew, several clever artists were making drawings

43

of the same people. You probably know many of the amusing pictures they drew, especially those of Cruikshank, Tenniel, and Du Maurier. If you wish to know how David and Peggotty and Betsy Trotwood and little Emily really looked, ask your librarian to show you some of the illustrations that these artists made. Because these pictures give the very best idea of how the people of Dickens' time looked, you might copy them for your marionettes. Their faces have a great deal of character, their clothes are those of that time, and they are so quaint and characteristic that they will never be uninteresting.

Probably the most beautiful marionette plays that one can imagine could be done from the great stories in the Bible. Just as in the early days of Christianity, when marionettes helped the people to see and feel the great scenes in their new religion, so, it would seem, that a time might come again when the little figures might return to their earliest uses. This could well be done in Christmas and Easter plays for the church and Sunday school. Imagine the story of Joseph and his brethren with scenes showing:

1. The tent life of Israel.
2. The kind old father.
3. The cruel brothers.
4. The selling into bondage.
5. The court life in Egypt.
6. Joseph among his new friends.
7. The famine.
8. The visit of the brothers.
9. The remorse of the brothers.
10. Joseph's forgiveness in the last scene.

44

Parables, such as that of the Good Samaritan, are full of dramatic possibilities.

How many beautiful plays appropriate for Christmas, Easter, and saints' days could be made from the lives of the saints! If you are interested in a play for your Sunday school or your parochial school, read and make into a play the life of Saint Christopher, Saint George, Saint Patrick, Saint Francis of Assisi, Saint Agnes, Saint Genevieve, Saint Catherine of Sienna, or Saint Joan of Arc.

If you love fairy tales you will, no doubt, wish to make a fairy marionette play. You probably know many of the books listed here:

Mother Goose
Hans Christian Andersen's Fairy Tales—Tr. Lucas
The Brothers Grimm Fairy Tales—Tr. Crane.
The Arabian Nights—Ed. Colum
Adventures of Nils—Lagerlöf
Gulliver's Travels—Swift
The Blue Bird—Maeterlinck
Water Babies—Kingsley
The Little Lame Prince—Craik
Old Peter's Russian Tales—Ransome
Aesop's Fables—Ed. Jacobs
Undine—La Motte—Fouqué
Story of the Rhinegold—Chapin
Japanese Fairy Book—Ozaki
Wonder Tales of China Seas—Olcott
Tales of Wonder—Wiggin and Smith

Here are a few familiar poems that may be turned into marionette plays:

Hiawatha—Longfellow
Evangeline—Longfellow

Marionettes—Masks and Shadows

Story Telling Ballads—Olcott
Lady of the Lake—Scott
Lays of Ancient Rome—Macaulay

Many other stories will, no doubt, occur to you, and many ways of turning them to your needs.

CHAPTER IV

Making Your Stage

A CHAIR, sofa, or table top may have been the first stage on which you moved about your tin soldiers and paper dolls. Your imagination supplied the

scenery and lighting. A small table turned upside down and placed on top of another table may have been your next invention. A curtain drawn about its three sides and your string of Christmas-tree lights gave you a very satisfactory little theater. As your stagecraft developed, you may have seen possibilities

in a soap box or a dry goods box. By knocking out one side to make a proscenium opening and painting scenery on the back of the box or on to cardboards which you slipped in and out, you had a very real stage. With a proscenium arch made from cardboard and decorated to suit the play, a little curtain on a rod, Christmas-tree lights, and your company of small doll actors, you had a complete theater. It could be placed in a door or an archway, or between two screens.

Possibly you were interested in the Burattini. You may have made a booth somewhat like the illustration and decorated it quite gaily. It had this advantage. By means of hinges it could be folded together. It was no trouble to take anywhere, indoors or out, to a friend's backyard, to school, to the playground, or even to a picnic.

If your enthusiasm had led you further, you would have been interested in the drawings of a semi-professional marionette stage which are shown on the next two pages.

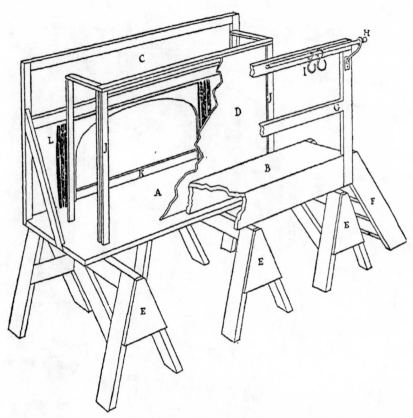

CONSTRUCTIONAL DRAWING OF MARIONETTE STAGE—BACK
VIEW—WITHOUT LIGHTING

A   *Stage floor, 10′ x 32″.*
B   *Bridge for puppeteers, 24″ wide, 12″ high above stage floor.*
C   *Beaverboard facing (10′ x 4′ 6″) in which proscenium arch*
      (6′ x 30″) is cut.
D   *Backdrop, 7′ x 4′.*
E   *Supporting trestles, 33″ high.*
F   *Bridge ladder. Two ladders are needed, one at each end of bridge.*
G   *Bridge fence.*
H   *Iron rod attached to fence for holding S hooks.*
I   *S hooks for holding marionettes when not in use.*
J   *Supporting frame for wings and backdrop.*
K   *Footlight trough.*
L   *Curtains.*

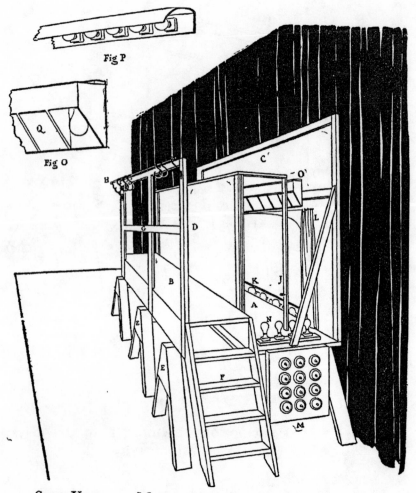

SIDE VIEW OF MARIONETTE STAGE—WITH LIGHTING

K   Footlights.
M   Switchboard.
N   Movable strip (one for each side of stage) of wing lights.
O   Boxed overhead lights for general stage illumination. Nine
        sections complete the line.
R   Large curtains between the audience and back stage—framing
        the stage.
Fig. O   Two sections of overhead lights showing bulb, and col-
        ored sheet gelatin Q inserted. Each section can be
        operated independently from the switchboard.
Fig. P   If the boxed lights are not practicable the simple tin
        trough with colored bulbs may be used.

CHAPTER V

Making Your Marionette

IN YOUR adventures with marionettes, probably nothing will give you more pleasure than the actual making of them. This is equally true of the Burattini, of the doll puppet, and of the real marionette.

The Burattini, Guignol, or Mitten puppet is the simplest kind of marionette. It is usually nothing more than a head, two arms, and an empty sack. The most important part of a Guignol is its head. This can be made from unbleached muslin, from a hollow doll's head, it can be carved out of a block of soft wood, or it can be made from papier-mâché.

Muslin Head. Here is a pattern for the unbleached muslin head. Sew the two halves together and then stuff firmly with cotton. If you dampen the cheeks, the muslin will stretch and then you can round them out with more cotton. Into the neck insert a cuff of stiff paper, $\frac{7}{8}$ of an inch in diameter. It should be fastened either by sewing or glueing. This cuff gives you space for the finger which manipulates the

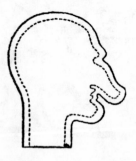

head. Water colors or crayons may be used for painting the face. Before you begin, experiment on scraps of muslin.

Doll's Head. If you wish to use the hollow head of a doll, you will probably find it necessary to remodel its features. This is done by taking papier-mâché, a mixture of bits of paper mixed with flour paste, and building out the nose, the cheeks, and the chin, in order to give them more character. The building out must be done gradually, a bit at a time, after you have made the surface rough by the use of sandpaper or a file. When you are sure that you have finished the head, stand twenty or thirty feet away from it and see if it is still interesting to you. This is an excellent test. Those in the last rows of your audience will be even farther away and your Burattini must hold their interest.

Wooden Head. Boys who like to whittle will enjoy carving out wooden heads. If you decide to carve the head from wood, use a soft wood, such as pine. Start with a piece about 5 inches long by $3\frac{1}{2}$ inches wide by $3\frac{1}{2}$ inches high. It is well to keep in mind that the head is egg shaped. The chin is the small end of the

egg. Observe that the eyes are placed halfway between the top of the head and the chin, and that the nose is placed halfway between the eyes and the chin. Notice, also, that the mouth is placed halfway between the nose and the chin. The illustration will show you how to go about the carving. Cut the big planes first, then the smaller planes. Curve the cheeks and chin if the character requires it. You will then be ready to drill the $\frac{7}{8}$ inch hole up into the neck. Into this hole is thrust the forefinger of the puppeteer.

Papier-mâché Head. If you wish to make a papier-mâché head for your Burattini, follow the directions for making the head of the true marionette which you will find on page 67.

Hair. For hair, use yarn, lamb's wool, or frayed hemp, as is best suited to the character. The toe of a stocking makes an excellent foundation for the wig, since it so perfectly fits the head. When the material for the hair has been sewed to this foundation, glue it to the head. When the glue has set, you can arrange the hair.

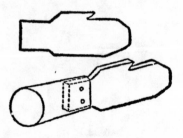

Hands. Burattini hands should be cut out of wood and shaped as in the illustration. Sandpapering makes them smooth. Little cuffs of cardboard should be glued or tacked onto the wrists in order to make a place for the thumb and second finger of the puppeteer.

Painting. When you have finished carving both the head and hands you are ready to paint them. You will need red, yellow, blue, and white oil paints. Use a piece of smooth wood or glass for a palette. Squeeze onto your palette a small amount of each color. As you know, people do not have pure-white skins. There is a tinge of yellow orange in the white man's skin, deep red and orange in that of the red man, brown in that of the Negro, and yellow in that of the Oriental. Begin by squeezing out onto your palette a small quantity of white paint. Only clowns' faces, however, are painted a pure white. You must add a bit of yellow and red to the white paint if you are painting a white man's face. If you are painting a red man's face, you must add more red and a bit of blue. For the face of an Oriental, add yellow to your white paint and the least bit of red and blue. For the black man's face, use black paint instead of white paint and into it mix a very small amount of orange and blue. Use a palette knife for mixing oil paints and turpentine for thinning them. Do not be timid when you begin to paint. Stong and vigorous painting is as important and necessary as strong and vigorous modeling in bringing out the features and expression. When the painting is finished, the face should fully express your idea of the character.

The Body. Now we come to the mantle or cloak which gives a kind of body to the Burattini. The illustration shows patterns for the front, back, and sleeves. To this foundation you can sew any costume that your character may require. The hands are fastened into the ends of the sleeves. When the cloak is fastened securely about the neck, it becomes a kind of sack, open only at the bottom. Now slip your hand inside this sack or mantle, your forefinger into the head, your thumb and second finger into the arms. The head will bow, the arms will move, and the little figure comes to life.

ANIMAL BURATTINI

Burattini animals can be made for such stories as *The Three Pigs*, *The Three Bears*, and *Little Red Riding Hood*. There are several ways of making them. The

A After completing papier-mâché head, cut out lower jaw as shown by dotted line. Then replace and paste a piece of thin muslin over lower cut, as shown by light line. This will not be seen when the head is painted.

B Dotted lines show the narrow elastic glued to upper and lower jaw. One piece on each side. The forefinger of the puppeteer pulls down the lower jaw, when it is released the elastic snaps the mouth shut.

first way is to use the head of an old toy animal. Into the center of this head cut a hole for the forefinger. Then attach this head to a suitable sack or coat. The forepaws of the animal can be fastened into the sleeves.

Another way is to carve the heads and paws out of soft wood. A third way is to cut them out of suitable cloth. A fourth way is to make them out of papier-mâché in the same way as the papier-mâché heads described on page 67. This illustration will show you how the lower jaw is cut out and then attached in such a way that the puppeteer can open and close the mouth.

Scale. Before you begin to make your marionette, you must decide upon the kind of stage you intend to use, for the size of the stage determines the size of the marionette. It is the right relation of the marionette to the stage that creates an illusion and makes your audience feel that the little figures are life-size. For the semi-professional stage, use a scale of $2\frac{1}{2}$ inches or 3 inches to the foot. If you use a scale of $2\frac{1}{2}$ inches to a foot, it would make a 15-inch marionette represent a 6-foot man. If you use a scale of 3 inches to a foot, your 6-foot hero would be represented by a marionette 18 inches high. Never forget your scale of measurements. All properties and stage settings must be worked out to the same scale you have fixed for your marionettes.

TURNING DOLLS INTO MARIONETTES

A very simple kind of marionette can be made from a ten- or fifteen-cent doll. Change the face as you did the Burattini face. Then take off the arms and legs and separate the arms at the elbows and the legs at the knees. Fasten the upper and lower arms together with tape. Do the same thing with the upper and

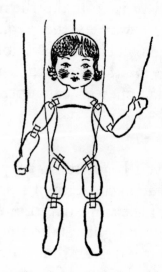

lower legs. Then fasten the arms and legs to the body as in the illustration. The tape gives free movement at the joints.

Strings. This type of marionette requires not more than seven strings: two for the shoulders, two for the hands, two for the knees, and one for the back. The shoulder string should be about 42 inches long. The other strings are longer as you can see in the illustration. Waxed black linen thread can be used for the strings.

Controllers. For this kind of marionette you can use either a horizontal-bar controller or a cross-bar controller. The illustration gives measurements and con-

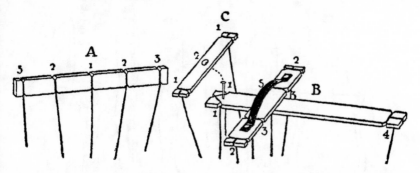

A *Horizontal-bar controller*
 1. *Back string*
 2. *Shoulder strings*
 3. *Hand strings*

B *Cross-bar controller*
 1. *Hand strings*
 2. *Head strings*
 3. *Shoulder strings*

 4. *Back strings*
 5. *Leather strap under*
  which the hand slips

C *Foot controller*
 1. *Foot strings*
 2. *Hole to slip over nail*
  in controller B when
  not in use.

struction, and indicates the place for attaching the strings.

STOCKING MARIONETTE

Another kind of marionette is made from old stockings or any soft material. The head and body are in one piece. Each arm is in one piece. Each leg is in two pieces. Cut and sew according to directions. Stuff the head very firmly with cotton. At the base of the neck leave a quarter of an inch between the two rows of stitching. This will permit the head to move. The body should be stuffed less firmly than the head, especially at the waistline, so that the figure can bend easily.

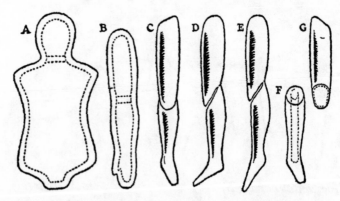

A Body pattern. Dotted line indicates stitching. Do not stitch
  across the bottom until after the stuffing has been inserted.
B Arm pattern. Dotted line indicates stitching.
C Front view of the leg stuffed, showing upper leg extending over
  lower leg. This is to prevent a forward swing at the knee.
D Side view of C showing the fastening; the upper leg is sewed to
  the lower leg at the back of the knee. Note the downward slant
  of the foot.
E A dancer's leg showing the downward drop of the toe.
F Lower leg showing round piece of wood to insure stiffness.
G Back view of upper leg. Dotted line indicates the piece of light-
  weight cardboard inserted to insure stiffness.

Note: Pieces of lead or small shot are used to weight the feet and
hands. A lead dress weight may be sewed in the torso to give the body
weight. Cotton or soft rags are used for the stuffing.

Staples. Into each side of the head, where the ears
would naturally come, insert a staple. It requires a
great deal of patience to insert these staples into this
kind of head but it can be done. Just where you place
these staples is very important. If you place them too
far forward the head will be drawn too far back when
the strings are attached to the staples. On the contrary, if the staples are inserted too far back, the

head will fall forward when suspended from the strings. If you wish to make a pompous, strutting character, then place the staples forward. If you wish to show a hunchback or bowed old age, then place the staples quite far back. Between these two extremes is the normal place for your staples.

Modeling. When the staples have been inserted, dip your fingers into water and dampen the head and then cover it with some kind of modeling clay that hardens when exposed to the air. The features of your character can be modeled with your fingers and the help of an orange stick or a toothpick. Do not cover the staples, for the headstrings must be attached to them later. This kind of marionette head should be painted with tempora colors or with oil paints. Paint the hands the same color as the face. When the paint is dry, cover the head with glue and attach the hair, which may be made from yarn, mercerized cotton, silk, or lamb's wool.

A marionette of this kind could be used on the semi-professional stage if it is carefully constructed, made to scale, and appropriately costumed. The strings are attached to the head staples, to the shoulders, the hands, the back, and to the knees. For this type of marionette use the cross-bar controller.

THE REAL MARIONETTE

The third type of marionette, which might be called the real marionette, is somewhat more complicated, but it is better suited to the larger stage and to more exacting plays. There is scarcely a thing that this type of marionette cannot be made to do if skilfully constructed. Its greater flexibility of neck, waist, wrist, and ankle makes it possible for it to bow, kneel, sit down, turn its head, dance, play a musical instrument, climb a wall, or perform any number of lively tricks.

CHARACTER

A marionette should be as individual as a human being, both in its appearance and in its character. Before you make your marionette, you must have clearly in mind the character you wish to portray. You should aim to make its appearance indicate its character. Let us suppose that you are about to make a marionette of Myles in *Men of Iron*. Let us make a list of his characteristics: brave, strong, loyal, daring, courageous. Now choose one of these traits which you think most fully sums up the character of Myles. Probably you will choose the word "courageous." The problem now is to create a marionette whose appearance will suggest the Myles who is brave, strong, loyal, daring, but, above all things, courageous. Can you not see him, tall, broad of shoulder, fearless of eye, as he stands before Sir James Lee? Strong of limb and strong of will, he reflects the spirit of his time. You now have the problem of creating out of a few bits of wood and cloth this daring, headstrong young squire.

Begin by making a working drawing somewhat like the illustration. Now make drawings of the face of Myles just as you imagine it, front view and side view. Always consider the age of the character you wish to model. Faces of the young are smooth and round, the brow unwrinkled; those of the middle aged less smooth and round, with the jaw, chin, and

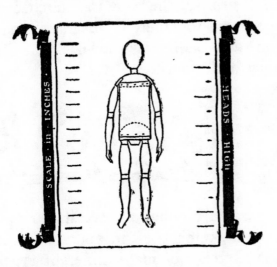

nose more clearly defined. In old age, sagging muscles produce lines and hollows around the eyes, nose, and mouth. You must also consider the structure of a face. This means giving attention to the shape of the jaw, chin, nose, lips, and the eye sockets. In modeling the face of Myles in *Men of Iron*, you would naturally give him a forceful chin and nose, and a large, firm mouth. If you were modeling Lady Alice in the same play, you would express her daintiness and lightness by giving her a delicate nose, smiling lips, rounded cheeks and chin. Lastly, you should study the expression of the face. Have you ever noticed what happens to the muscles around the mouth when a person smiles or is sad or angry? When we smile the muscles lift the corners of the mouth upward; when we are sad the mouth droops at the corners; when we are angry our lips become straight and firmly set. The brow is very tell-tale and can show different moods. In surprise, the brows are arched. Curiosity draws the brows together, anger draws them together and downward. Sadness is shown by the drooping of both brows and mouth.

If you are to become a successful puppet maker, keep a small sketch book in your pocket and make numerous sketches of many different types of faces and of human figures.

Modeling. With your drawings before you, take a lump of clay or plasticine and model it into the general egg shape of the head. The small end will represent the chin. The large end will represent the crown of the head. Add the clay for the neck. Draw a light line on the clay to locate the brow, the length of the nose, and the position of the mouth. Now while you hold this egg-shaped head in your hands, place your thumbs just below the line of the brow, and gently and firmly press the clay down and out and up to form the eye sockets. Then build up the nose and lips.

It is unnecessary to model the ears. In the first stages of your modeling, you cannot expect the head to resemble your ideal character, because you will be striving for the general proportions of the face. When once you have attained these proportions you can then begin to work for a likeness. Besides your ten fingers, you may find an orange stick or a sharpened match a valuable tool.

Making a Mold. After you have finished the head it is necessary to make a plaster of Paris mold of it. One way to do this is to take a small cardboard box that will hold the head and allow an inch of space on all six sides. Grease the box on the inside with vaseline. At the same time grease thoroughly and evenly with a brush the clay or plasticine head. Now mix about one half pint of plaster of Paris with enough water to give it the consistency of thick cream. This must be done with quickness, for the hardening process cannot be stopped once it has set in. Pour this mixture into the greased box until it is half full. Then place the head, back down, into the plaster. Allow fifteen to thirty minutes for the plaster of Paris to harden. Now grease the exposed surface of the clay or plasticine head. Mix more plaster with water and cover the face thoroughly. Allow this to stand overnight. The next day, when you remove the box, the two halves of the plaster cast can be separated. Out will fall the clay or plasticine head, which you will no longer need because you now have the two molds for making the papier-mâché head.

A simpler way to make the mold is this: Mark the clay as in the illustration. Then insert pieces of tin or stiff paper, such as oak tag. When the clay is dry,

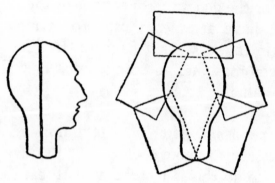

apply a coat of vaseline to it and to the tin or paper. Then apply the plaster of Paris and keep applying it until you think it is fully an inch thick. After the plaster hardens, proceed in the same manner with the other side of the head. When both sides are hard, separate them from the clay and you will have two molds.

Papier-mâché. You are now ready to make the papier-mâché heads. Begin by making a small quantity of flour paste. Take two heaping tablespoonfuls of flour and mix with cold water to the consistency of cream, add two cups of hot water, place over fire and stir constantly until it comes to the boiling point and boil for two minutes. A few drops of oil of cloves will keep the paste fresh in hot weather.

Now tear wrapping paper into small strips about five inches long. Soak them in water for a few minutes, then wring out and dip into the flour paste. Take a piece and rub it gently between the fingers until the paper feels like wet chamois skin. Then press it into the back of the mold for the head. Continue to cover the surface with piece after piece. If necessary, you may tear the paper into smaller pieces. There must not be a wrinkle, but the pieces should overlap slightly. In this way you cover the entire surface with paper of one color. For the second layer use paper of another color. For the third layer use the first color, and so on, alternately, through the fifth layer. This alternation of colors will help you to keep account of the layers, and insures uniform thickness. Allow the edges of the paper to extend over the edges of the mold.

Do the same thing with the mold for the face, but use much more care to see that every depression is smoothly and evenly filled in order to bring out the features properly. The paper should stay in the mold until dry. The two halves of the head and neck can then easily be removed. The edges should be trimmed off. The two halves can be held together and fastened with strips of papier-mâché.

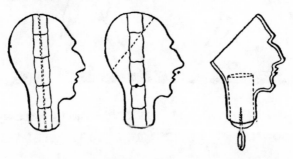

When you have finished making the head, cut out the crown as you see in the illustration. A round stick

an interesting problem. Two boys asked to be responsible for the horses in *Men of Iron*. They went downtown and looked about in the toy departments of the largest stores until they found two wooden toy horses exactly in scale with the 15-inch marionettes which were to be used in this play. They began by taking the horses off their wheeled platforms. These toy horses were very stiff. In order to enable them to move their heads, necks, and legs, it was first necessary to saw off the heads, necks, upper and lower legs.

The drawing shows the way these parts were again attached so that great freedom of movement was possible.

For the bear marionette, a teddy bear was used. Since a teddy bear is very stiff, it was necessary to remove all the stuffing from the head, body, and legs. In order to make the head drop forward, the snout was weighted with a small three-cornered sack of shot. The paws were also weighted in order to make the bear stand naturally. The bear was very lightly restuffed. The strings were attached to each side of the head, to the shoulders, lower part of the back, and to each of the four paws. The marionette was re-weighted no less than four times, in order to get the right balance to make its movements seem natural and bearlike.

A girl was responsible for the three doves used in the second scene of *Men of Iron*. She decided upon the proper scale and then cut a pattern for the body and another for the wings. The body she made from soft gray silk and weighted it near the tail. The wings were wired along their upper edges and then attached to the body. Each dove required three strings, one for the center of the back and one for the tip of each wing.

In the *Adventures of Alice*, it was necessary to have a caterpillar, a frog footman, a Cheshire cat, a pig baby, a dormouse, and a March hare. The Tenniel illustrations for *Alice in Wonderland* and *Through the Looking Glass* were closely followed. The students who made these animals tried to give to each one the character which it had in the story. The heads of the caterpillar, the frog footman, and the March hare were first modeled in clay. Molds were then made from these modeled heads. Then papier-mâché heads were made in just the same way as the papier-mâché heads of the true marionettes. To the papier-mâché head of the caterpillar was attached a body. Nile-green silk was used for the upper part and yellow-green silk for the under part. Half hoops of dress cord were stitched to the under side of the back, in order to indicate the segments. A rubber tube for smoke passed through the body from mouth to tail. Because the caterpillar was almost human, he was given hands and arms. The frog footman had a frog's head, throat, and webbed hands, and the body of a footman.

The March hare had the head and forepaws of a hare and the body of a country gentleman. He was made to appear rather simple, credulous and bland. He had great ears, side burns, and an engaging air, which belied his occasional impatience. The white rabbit was brisk and dapper. He was conscious of his shell-pink ears, fetching whiskers, and the large elegant watch which he drew from his pocket with a flourish.

Marionette animals such as dogs, cats, and pigs may be made from cloth. Even dragons may be made from cloth. Every animal marionette presents a new problem for your ingenuity to solve.

The directions and suggestions which are given in this chapter are meant to guide and to help you. However, it will be your own experiments and inventions which will give you the greatest satisfaction and lead you on to new achievements in the art of puppet-making.

CHAPTER VI

Making Your Scenery

THE stage is made. The puppets have a floor to walk upon. Is anything more required? You say, "Oh, yes, there must be scenery before it will be a real stage." Who shall plan and make this scenery? Shall this be the work of one pupil or the work of the whole group? All will want a share in it. This means that the large group should be divided into smaller groups and that each group should be made responsible for a scene.

Let us suppose you have dramatized Howard Pyle's *Men of Iron* and made a play of four scenes. In order to give the same note of unity to the scenery that you are trying to give to your play, every scene must be in harmony with every other scene and with the whole idea of the play.

Three scenes of *Men of Iron* are laid in Devlen Castle, England. What do we know about castles and about English castles? When were castles built? We go to the library and find books that give us both illustrations and descriptions. In one of these, Quennell's *History of Everyday Things in England*, there are drawings and descriptions of castles of the XIth, XIIth, XIIIth, XIVth, and XVth centuries. The story of *Men of Iron* is laid in the year 1400. Devlen Castle had probably seen many generations of the Mackworth family come and go long before this time. It probably was built in the XIIIth or early XIVth century. Let us follow, therefore, the plan of a XIVth Century castle. On page 86, we find a ground plan and a picture of such a castle. Read the description of its massive stone walls and towers, colorless and gray, and of its courtyard and great hall. The first scene of the play is laid in the courtyard. The second scene is laid in the ladies' garden. The third is laid in the great hall.

Your problem now is to give your audience a picture of this castle, and the varied life of its courtyard, its ladies' garden, and its great hall. On a stage measuring 30 inches by 55 inches, how can this be done? If the settings are wisely planned, the audience will have such a vivid impression of the courtyard, the garden, and the castle, that they will feel they are living in the time of the play.

You may be interested in the way a group of boys and girls planned the stage settings for this play. The first scene was laid in the courtyard. Instead of trying to show every little incident and detail of the life of the courtyard, every stable and blacksmith shop, every well and water trough, they asked themselves what important things happened in this first act and listed them as follows: First, Myles practised at the pels. Second, the armorer worked in his shop. Third,

Myles played with the squire, and threw a ball over the wall. Then they took the ground-floor plan of the XIVth century castle, as they found it in the book, studied it carefully, and planned this setting. Every stage setting must give the actors enough room to

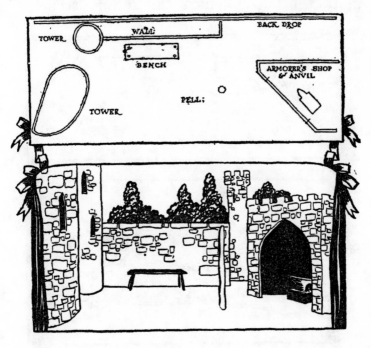

move about in. It must have exits. It must be a well-composed picture. It must be related to the scene that follows. You can readily see how this careful planning met each of these requirements: First, it gave room for their puppets to do what they were required to do. Second, it gave them the two necessary exits, one into the castle, the other out to the drawbridge. Third, it made, by the arrangement of wall, towers, and armorer's shop, a well-composed picture.

Fourth, by this arrangement of the first scene, they were able to carry the imagination of the audience, with Myles, when he climbed over the wall, into the ladies' garden, in the second scene.

Another group planned the second scene. They

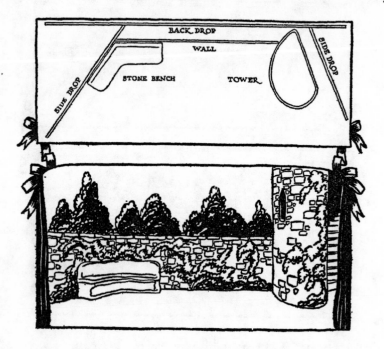

imagined themselves on the inside of the garden, on the other side of the wall shown in the first scene. They asked themselves, not what do we see, but what happens in the garden during this scene.

First, Lady Anne plays a lute and Lady Alice dances.

Second, Myles tumbles over the wall.

Third, the Earl of Mackworth comes from the castle and returns into the castle.

Here is the plan they made. You can see how they planned first to have plenty of floor space for Lady Alice's dance, and then, to keep the wall away from the back drop so that Myles could climb over it. Second, it provided the necessary exit. Third, through the arrangement of ivy-covered towers, trellised wall, and garden bench, it made a charming picture. Fourth, by means of the exit into the castle, the interest of the audience was carried into the third scene.

Still another group planned the third scene which

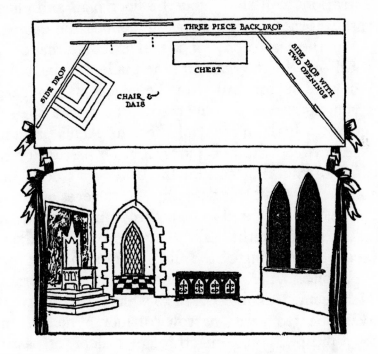

is laid in the great hall of the castle. Their purpose was to make the audience feel the spaciousness of the great hall and of its galleries and corridors. Again it was necessary to think of what happened in this scene. The first difficulty to present itself was this: How can enough space be provided for eleven puppets to be on the stage at the same time, to move about freely and moreover keep the stage picture beautiful? A clever boy thought of making a gallery at the side for Lady Anne and Lady Alice to sit in. This gave them a place in the picture and enabled their puppeteers to stand behind the wings of the bridge. Here they were out of the way of the other nine puppeteers who stood on the bridge behind the back drop. These illustrations will show you the floor plan and elevations. Another boy ingeniously planned the doorway seen in the elevation, for a rear exit. He made two back drops. In the rear drop he made a stained-glass window. The forward drop he made in two parts. As you can see in the illustration, he placed one section just a little in front of the other. This provided space between the two parts, for the passage of the strings of the king and all the other characters that should enter from this doorway. To the eyes of the audience there appeared to be no break in the wall above the doorway, neither did the eyes of the audience detect the painting of the tiled floor on the rear back drop, done in perspective, another bit of cleverness, which seemed to give width to what otherwise would have appeared a very narrow corridor. Whenever one sees a puppet going out through a door, or passing by outside a window, he is interested, because it gives the suggestion of life and activity beyond the stage.

You have a chance to show yourselves artists in the placing of doorways and windows. Doorways that open upon courtyards, or that give glimpses of distant landscapes, and windows that open out upon gardens, are charming details when appropriately used. Avoid, if possible, painting doors and windows on to your scenery.

The group that made the tournament scene had the problem of providing plenty of space for the puppet

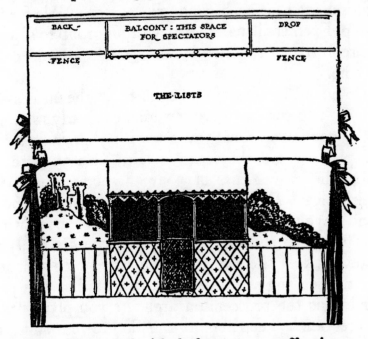

spectators. It was decided that a very effective scene could be made by placing the royal box, for the king and his court, at the rear of the stage. Directly in front of the box there was space enough for the tournament. The entrances for this scene were on the right and left, and were large enough to admit the horses and their riders. On the back drop was painted a landscape of the surrounding country, with hills, trees, and a distant castle. It usually happens that certain members of a large group are more drawn to one scene than to another. If there are too many in one group, some pupils, realizing the importance of equalizing the size of the groups, will, good-naturedly, turn to the assistance of the smaller groups. There should be boys and girls in each group, and a chairman selected for each, who will be responsible for his group. Each chairman meets with his group to discuss the requirements, general arrangement, and the color scheme.

Do not be in a hurry to begin. Have the impression you wish to convey to your audience clearly in mind. Close your eyes. Can you see with your mind's eye the place where the scene is laid? Can you see its color, the movements of your characters, and hear their voices? Does the picture which comes to your mind's eye put you into the mood which you felt when you first read the story? If it does, you are ready to begin. Take a sheet of paper about 14 by 17 inches. Let the rectangle you draw on this be the same proportion as the proscenium arch. As you plan within this rectangle, keep in mind the picture your audience is going to see when your scene is presented.

When the plans for a scene have been submitted, choose the best one, or put all the best ideas into a new plan. Remember, if you understand proportion, everything is possible. You can show lofty cliffs that seem to tower into the air. You can show level plains that seem to stretch miles to the horizon.

When you have finished your plan for each scene,

you are ready for your tools and materials. Here is a list of the things usually required:

Tools	Materials
Rulers	Beaver board
Scissors	Wood
Hammers	Unbleached muslin
Brushes	Burlap
Saws, large and very small	Tacks, nails
Screw driver	Screws
Dye pans	Dyes
	Gesso
	Glue (flake and liquid)
	Oil colors
	Water colors by the pound

Suppose that you belong to the first group. Take your plan and place it before you. For the back drop, wall, and wing, you may use beaver board, heavy paper, canvas, or muslin stiffened by a thin coat of boiled starch. Now go to your stage and measure the height and width of the back drop and the wing frames. Then cut out the back drop and wing from the material you have chosen. Place these in their positions on the stage. Take a piece of charcoal, or soft lead pencil, and lightly sketch your design onto the back drop and wing. Now step back, at least ten feet, in order to see if your arrangement, perspective, and scale are correct. You may find that your distant tower is too large or too small, or that your trees are too small or too tall, or that your arrangement is not according to your well-worked-out plan. Make your corrections. Then take the back drop and wing from the stage, and lay them flat on desks or tables. With your scenery in this position carefully complete your sketch.

Now take a piece of white chalk and draw on the stage floor the ground plan. If the tower nearest the front is made large, and the one farther away slightly smaller, you will get the effect of distance. You will observe that the larger tower is not round, although it appears so to the audience. By making it flat at the back, you gain floor space for the marionettes that may be waiting to go on the stage. The bases and tops of these towers are of wood; the sides are of strips of wood which serve as a foundation for the burlap cover. The armorer's shop, too, may be made of wood and beaver board. The effect of stone may be produced by covering the surface of these towers, walls, and shop with a mixture of sand and gesso.

Colors. When you are ready to paint the scenery, you can use ordinary house paints, showcard colors, or water colors. House paints are ready mixed. Water colors are practical and inexpensive when bought in powder form, but when you use them you should add several tablespoonfuls of a fixative made from flake glue dissolved in water. Various kinds of showcard colors are clear and pure and very easy to use, but they are comparatively expensive. If you cannot afford many colors buy red, yellow, dark blue, and white. By combining them you can get a wide range of colors. If you are not limited in the amount you can spend, add to your list orange, light green, light blue, mauve, and magenta.

Color Mixing. You probably know something about color and the mixing of colors. However, you may find the following directions helpful. First let us experiment with yellow. If you add a very little bit of blue to the yellow you can see the yellow turning to greenish-yellow. As you gradually add more blue you can see the greenish-yellow turning to yellow-green and finally to green.

Let us begin again with pure yellow. If you add a very little bit of red to the yellow you can see the yellow turning to orange-yellow. As you gradually add more red, you can see the orange-yellow turning to yellow-orange and finally to orange.

Let us begin once more with pure yellow. If you add a very little bit of blue and red to the yellow, you can see the yellow turning to a grayish-yellow. As you gradually add more blue and red you can see the grayish-yellow turning to yellowish-gray, and finally turning to a neutral gray.

Let us experiment with red. If you add a little bit of yellow to the red you can see the red turning to yellowish-red. As you gradually add more you can see the yellowish-red turning to reddish-orange, and finally to orange.

Let us begin again with pure red. If you add a very little bit of blue to the red you can see the red turning to a bluish-red. As you gradually add more blue you can see the bluish-red turning to reddish-purple and finally to purple.

Let us begin once more with pure red. If you add a very little bit of yellow and blue to the red you can see

94

the red turning to a grayish-red. As you gradually add more yellow and blue you can see the grayish-red turning to reddish-gray and finally turning to a neutral gray.

Let us experiment with blue. If you add a little bit of yellow to the blue you can see the blue turning to greenish-blue. As you gradually add more yellow you can see the greenish-blue turning to bluish-green and finally to green.

Let us begin again with pure blue. If you add a very little bit of red to the blue you can see the blue turning to a reddish-blue. As you gradually add more red you can see the reddish-blue turning to bluish-purple and finally to purple.

Let us begin once more with pure blue. If you add a very little bit of yellow and red to the blue you can see the blue turning to a grayish-blue. As you gradually add more yellow and red you can see the grayish-blue turning to bluish-gray and finally turning to a neutral gray.

Brown, which is not a pure color, is made by adding a little blue to orange. There are yellow-browns and red-browns, but some blue is used in making every one of them.

Value and Intensity. What do these technical terms: "Color Value" and "Color Intensity" mean to you? There is a certain satisfaction in understanding their meanings and in being able to use them correctly. Value refers to the amount of light reflected by a color. Light red is lighter in value than dark red. A color is always made lighter in value by the addition of white. Intensity refers to the strength or brilliancy of a color. Pure red is intense. When a little yellow or blue is added to it, it becomes a grayish-red, and consequently is less intense. If white is added to pure red, its intensity is lessened.

Brushes. For the painting of the scenery you will need several brushes of different sizes, varying in width from the small sable brush to the inch or inch and a half bristle brush. Use large brushes whenever possible. Work from left to right, using horizontal strokes or vertical downward strokes. Brushes are expensive, and should be given excellent care and thoroughly cleaned after using.

Let us suppose that you are ready to paint the scenery for *Men of Iron.* Let us take Scene I: what is the time of year and what is the hour of the day? You answer, "It is a day of sunshine, in early spring." Spring skies are clear and may be painted light blue; the trees may be painted yellow-green with splashes of pure yellow to give an effect of sunlight. The castle towers, wall, and armor shop, should be painted a warm neutral gray. An occasional touch of darker gray at the top of wall, windows, and tower suggests thickness and adds to the illusion you are creating. The distant castle tower on the back drop should be painted a lighter gray because it is far away.

In the second scene, the time of year is midsummer, and the time of day is mid-afternoon. Therefore, the sky was painted a deeper blue than that of the first scene. The trees were painted a richer green; the flowers were painted in brilliant colors. The castle walls and towers were painted a yellowish-gray, while the vines that clambered over them were painted a rich green. In order to carry the imagination of the audience into the castle, a circling stairway was painted on the right wing. The audience caught a glimpse of this stairway at the right of the tower.

In the third scene, which is laid in the great hall, the back drop, wings, and walls were painted a lighter gray than the outside walls. Sand and gesso were mixed with the gray paint in order to give the suggestion of rough stone. The great stone walls, as you know, made the old castles cold and colorless. This coldness was relieved by stained-glass windows, rich tapestries, hangings, and colorful costumes.

The boy who painted the tapestry for this scene went to books and to the old tapestries in the art museum for his inspiration. He produced the effect of rich tapestry by painting directly on the beaver board, with thin vertical strokes of pure color. Another student produced the effect of stained glass by making a design on tracing paper, painting it on both sides with water colors, and then fastening it to the window opening in the back drop. Manila, Haytol, or oak tag paper may be used instead of tracing paper; you can make them translucent by brushing both sides with a little linseed oil after the water colors are dry. A light placed behind these stained-glass windows brings out their designs and colors.

In the fourth act, which is the tournament scene, the time of year is late summer, the time of day is late afternoon. On the back drop was painted a landscape of the surrounding country, hills, trees, and a distant castle. The sky was painted a pale gold to signify the success of Myles in the combat. The royal box and fence were painted a dark earth brown. The box was enriched with gold and colorful hangings.

These directions are not meant to be followed. They are merely offered as suggestions, to assist you in meeting the problems your play may present. Every boy and girl ought to feel free enough, in every phase of his work, to express his own ideas. This should be equally true in arranging or writing a play, in making a marionette, in planning and constructing properties and scenery, and in experimenting with lighting. Few pleasures in life compare with the pleasure of creating something. In planning your scenery, much depends upon the plan and the type of stage you have chosen. No matter what the play or what the stage, you can make no mistake if you keep your backgrounds simple. Some of the greatest artists use no scenery. They produce their effects simply by means of curtains and lighting. Begin your experiment by using curtains. A light gray curtain for a back drop and the sides of your stage can give many charming effects, as you will discover when you begin experimenting with colored lights.

Few things will show your judgment and good taste more than your scenery, which must be first, last, and always, a background for the marionettes. This

Scenes from the Marionette play, "Men of Iron."

means that it must be either lighter or darker than the puppets, so that they can be seen against it. It must be so simple that the eye can follow the marionette easily, and not be lost in the detail of the background, which will happen if there are too many colors, and the colors are not of the same value. The scenery should not be an end in itself, but should be a beautiful setting for the marionettes, and by its fitness give an added sense of the beauty of your play.

So far we have not thought of the frame for our stage, which is called the proscenium, nor have we spoken of the stage curtains. These are important because they are what might be called an introduction to the play. If they strike the right note, they may even hold the thread of interest between the acts. It is usual to have a contrast between the proscenium and the curtains, and between the proscenium and the several settings of the play. If your play has several brightly lighted scenes, you will probably find that a gray proscenium with a very simple, appropriate design looks much better than a brightly colored one with elaborate designs. Use the same good taste in framing your stage picture as you would in framing any other picture. Grays, yellows, and dull gold are always pleasing. The best material to use for the curtains is unbleached muslin. Because it takes dye so beautifully, it sometimes comes to have the look of the richest old velvet. It should be thoroughly soaked in hot water and then rubbed between the hands before dipping in the dye bath. The selvedges should be gathered together and then the entire piece should be wrung out. The dye bath should be ready. If you wish a plain color you may dip the entire piece, usually four yards, two for each curtain, at one time. If, however, you wish to have the curtains darker at the bottom than at the top, you must allow the lower part to remain longer in the dye bath. As you gain experience in dyeing, you may wish to use two or even three different dyes for your curtains. The curtains for *Sigurd, the Volsung,* kept the same color symbolism as the costumes. The upper part was yellow to symbolize the wisdom of Odin, running into orange to symbolize the home ties of the Volsung line, and into deep red at the bottom, symbolizing the valor and courage of the hero, Sigurd. The curtains for *Men of Iron* were red at the top to symbolize the valor of Myles, then purple to symbolize the royal blood of the Mackworths, black at the bottom to symbolize the deceit, overthrow, and death of the Earl of Alban. Until you have acquired skill in dyeing it is best to hold to very simply colored curtains. These may be either in harmony with or in contrast to the color you have chosen for the proscenium. The curtains should never be ironed. They

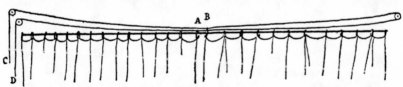

How to pull your curtains. Attach central ring of one curtain at A and the central ring of the other at B. Pulling string C closes the curtains, while D opens them.

should be smoothed out with the hands, when the muslin is still very damp, then hung up to dry. Hem carefully at the top and bottom, fold into pleats at the top. Small brass rings should then be sewed on to every pleat for the curtain strings to pass through. To the bottom of the curtain small dress weights should be fastened every five or six inches just under each curtain ring. Crease the folds with your hands. Your curtain may come to have its own way of looking just right—of behaving properly when it has its part to do, and may add the last note of craftsmanship and perfection to your scenery.

CHAPTER VII

Making Your Properties

PUPPETS usually require a few well-chosen properties. These should be in scale with the puppets, and serve some practical need. Properties should be similar to the things used in the time of your play, in the country of your play, and by the class or classes of people represented in your play.

It is well to be familiar with the life, customs, and manners of the people who lived at the time of your play. The library, historical museum, and art museum are sources of information. First, there is the library in which there are always books and pictures and a wealth of information for your use. Take several pieces of tracing paper with you when you go there, also several well-sharpened pencils, and your colored crayons. When you find a suitable illustration, make a sketch or a tracing of it and careful color notes.

Let us suppose that you are about to make the properties for *Men of Iron*. Take the story and from it make a list of the properties that you will need. You will probably make a list somewhat like this:

Act. I—Courtyard. Properties required:
  1. Bench for the squires to sit upon and later for Myles to stand upon.
  2. An upright post, or pell, to be used by Myles when he practises with his sword.
  3. An anvil to be placed in the armorer's shop.
  4. A ball for Myles.

Act II—Garden. Properties required:
  1. Garden seat for Lady Anne to sit upon when she plays her lute.
  2. A lute for Lady Anne.
  3. A ball for Myles.

Act III—Great Hall. Properties required:
  1. Throne for the king to sit upon.
  2. A dais for the throne to rest upon.
  3. A seat for the minstrel.
  4. A carved oak chest, such as was usually seen in the great halls.
  5. Royal carpet.
  6. Hangings for the ladies' gallery.
  7. A lute for the minstrel.

Act IV—The tournament. Properties required:
  1. A royal box.
  2. A fence.

The bench in Scene I was made of wood and was a copy of a picture of an English XVth Century bench.

Sometimes there are properties and effects that take special ingenuity and skill. Many boys have unusual ability in solving these problems. In the first scene of *Men of Iron* an anvil was needed. One boy asked to be responsible for the anvil. There was a miniature anvil in the classroom that had been used the year before by the class that had given *Sigurd, the Volsung*. Now, what did he do? First, he drilled two holes into the top of the anvil and placed a strip of mica on the iron between the holes. Then he attached a thin coil of wire, about the size of that in an electric toaster, screwed it down into the holes, where it met the charged wires which came up through the holes in the anvil. When the current was turned on, the coil glowed red. This boy also made a hammer, which he fastened in the hand of the puppet armorer. From the hammer a long wire stretched upward to the controller, and then down behind the scenes to the socket. When the armorer struck the anvil with his hammer, brilliant sparks flew in every direction. Care was

taken to strike the broad surface of the anvil top and to avoid striking the coil of wire. You will notice that he placed the mica and coil close to the edge, in order to give the armorer plenty of room for the strokes of his hammer.

The garden bench in Act II was made by a pupil who had made a special study of gardens. When one of the boys found that a lute was needed for this scene, he went to the art museum where he had the good fortune to find two lutes, a large one and a small one, both of Italian make. He then went to the historical museum where he found pictures of similar lutes used in England, in the time of his play. He now decided to use the large lute in the museum as a model for the lute of his minstrel, and the smaller one for Lady Alice. He then made careful drawings to scale, proceeded to carve the instruments from wood, and to stain them, and enrich them with gold. When they were finished, with the little detail of strings, they were such an exquisite note of perfection that they added much to the beauty of the scene, and gave a thrill of delight to all who saw them.

In Act III, a Gothic throne and a Gothic chest were needed. The boy who was responsible for these went to the art museum to look for Gothic furniture. He found a Gothic chest, and adapted its proportions and design to both the throne and the chest. He copied a XVth Century stool for the minstrel to sit upon. The carpet and hangings for this scene were made from large scraps of rich crimson velvet given by a generous upholsterer.

In Act IV, the royal box was historically true, as it was made from drawings of a royal box found in an old illuminated manuscript. It was constructed from wood and beaver board. Tapestries hung from the front of the box and pennants from tall poles at the corners.

Sometimes, when scenery has been especially well designed, it makes properties almost unnecessary.

For instance, in the throne room of King Elf in *Sigurd, the Volsung* the background is a dark, richly colored tapestry. Against this was placed the throne on a raised dais. With this single property the scene was a satisfying picture. When the three fair-haired maidens, dressed in white and gold, with flowing veils of pale rose, came to present the baby Sigurd to King Elf, it was a lovely picture.

The materials used for making properties are usually wood, cardboard, tacks, glue, ½-inch linen or cotton tape, papier-mâché, gesso, and paints. The tools needed are hammer, coping saw, scissors, and a sharp knife. Drawings should be kept before the worker for constant reference. They are his guide for proportion, design, and scale.

Accidents are as likely to happen in puppet families and at puppet parties as they are to happen in our homes and at our own parties. If the chairs are unsteady and the tables too light, they may cause trouble and embarrassment. Think what might have happened at Bob Kratchet's Christmas party in Charles Dickens' *Christmas Carol*, when all the puppets sat down to the well-laden table, if some thought had not been given to making it secure. How do you imagine this was done? The table and all the chairs were glued to a large piece of cardboard. When the scene was set, this was placed on the stage. In the time of Bob Kratchet, just as in our own time, houses contained many pieces of furniture and other things of daily use. Imagine what would happen, if we made all the properties that are mentioned in the story and then tried to crowd them on to the stage. There would be no room for the puppets to move about in. Our eyes would be confused with details and the picture would be ruined. Here is a list of the properties that were chosen by the group of children who gave *The Childhood of David Copperfield:*

Act   I. Sitting room in the Copperfield house
      An armchair for Peggotty
      A table for Peggotty and work basket
      Stool for little David
      Curtains for the windows

Act II. In the boathouse
      A chair for Peggotty
      A chair for Mrs. Gummidge
      A table for Peggotty's work basket and balls of bright-colored wool.
      A chest for David and Emily to sit upon
      A small box for Ham
      A chest of drawers, on top of the drawers a tray, teapot, two cups, and saucers
      Curtains for the windows

Act III. The seashore
      A log for David to sit upon
      A large rock for Emily to sit upon
      Two or three small rocks to complete the picture

Act IV. The schoolroom
      Six benches for the schoolboys
      Two desks, one for the master, one for his assistant
      Two chairs
      Books for the desks

Act V. Betsy Trotwood's garden
      A long bench where David rested
      A large kite for old Master Dick
      Three or four flower pots to complete the picture

Nearly all properties need some decoration. Some need color, others need merely stain. Occasionally it is necessary to give the effect of carved wood. This is necessary in plays of the Middle Ages like *Sigurd, the Volsung,* and *Men of Iron,* where your properties represent old wood carving. Gesso may be used to suggest this carving. Gesso was used by the craftsmen of the Middle Ages, especially in Italy, for enriching surfaces. This is the formula for making it: 2 tablespoons of varnish, 12 tablespoons of glue (best quality), 8 tablespoons of linseed oil. Mix these three ingredients together and allow to stand. In a separate dish put 20 rounded tablespoons full of whiting and then mix with water until it is the consistency of thick cream. Pour this into your first mixture and cook in a double boiler for ten minutes, stirring constantly. Then pour into a bottle and cork tightly. The gesso is now ready for use.

Work out your design and then draw it carefully upon the chair, chest, or throne which you mean to decorate. Apply the gesso with a small brush. Be very careful to keep well within the line of your design. The gesso will give you a pattern in relief. You must keep each surface flat for at least 12 hours, or until dry. If the design is not high enough when it is dry, a second coat may be applied. When you have covered all the parts which are to be painted and the gesso is dry, rub it over with a bit of oil paint mixed in these proportions: $\frac{3}{4}$ of ivory black, $\frac{1}{4}$ of burnt sienna thinned with a little turpentine. After the oil paint has dried, add a coat of dull finishing wax and rub down.

A fountain is a most effective and beautiful device. When placed in a garden, surrounded by miniature ferns and flowers, with birds singing, and soft colored lights playing upon its jetting water, it makes a scene of enchantment. Fountains are very simply

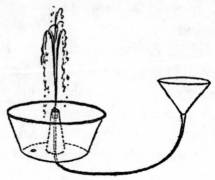

made as you can see in this illustration. A low cake tin, with a hollow tin centerpiece, a funnel, and a piece of $\frac{3}{4}$-inch rubber tubing about six feet long, are the only materials necessary.

Occasionally there is a need for smoke. In the play of *Aladdin and the Wonderful Lamp*, the genii appear out of a cloud of smoke. In *Sigurd, the Volsung*, the dragon may be made to breathe forth smoke. In the *Adventures of Alice*, you may remember the old caterpillar who sits on a toadstool and smokes his pipe. Smoke can be made from ammonia and hydrochloric acid. The illustration shows how this is done. In order to make the dragon breathe forth smoke, a rubber tube was run through its body from mouth to tail. The end that extended from the tail was connected with the tube that came from the bottles. When a boy blew through the tube,

smoke came from the dragon's mouth. In the marionette play of *Aladdin and His Wonderful Lamp,* a
hole was bored through the stage floor at the spot

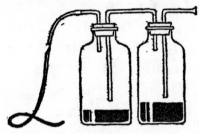

where the genie was to appear. At the clap of thunder
that announced the genie's appearance, a cloud of
smoke poured forth.

In the *Adventures of Alice,* when the caterpillar
was made, a tube was run through his body from tail
to mouth. When this tube was attached to the bottle
tube, and the lazy old fellow took his pipe in his
mouth, he appeared to blow out great puffs of smoke
to the surprise and delight of everyone.

The toadstool was such a nice property that you
may wish to know how it was constructed. The girl
who made it found some beautiful pictures of toad-
stools in an old number of the *National Geographic.*
She chose one of interesting shape and color as her
model, and reproduced it with papier-mâché. When
it was quite dry, she colored it to represent the
illustration. It was winter time when this play was
given. Had it been any other season, she could have
gone to the woods and fields and searched out a
beautiful specimen which would have served her purpose much better than the illustration.

Fireplaces and stoves are comparatively modern inventions. Braziers were used in earlier times. They consisted of a metal tripod and a basin to hold the coals. A brazier could be used appropriately in a Greek or Roman play, or in a play of the Middle Ages. The tripod could be made of wire or of tin. The basin could be made of tin, wood, or papier-mâché. Both the tripod and the basin should be painted to imitate bronze or iron. A tiny red bulb can be fastened into the center of the basin, and attached to a wire leading down from the tripod, through the stage floor. Slightly conceal the bulb with small bits of wood. The warm light from this brazier will throw a glow on the face of a marionette, who is warming his hands over it.

A marionette may carry a lantern. This marionette lantern may be made from any small tin or cardboard box. Find some pictures of old lanterns suitable for your play, and then make a lantern as much like the illustration as you can. A pattern of holes should be punched in the sides. A tiny electric bulb may be fastened inside the lantern and its wire carried up to the controller and from there to the battery.

Properties should be made in a craftsmanlike way. A craftsman respects his materials and his tools. He cleans his brushes and palette as soon as he finishes the work of the day, and puts his materials in order for the next day's work. He never hurries. His reward is his satisfaction in the excellence of his work.

CHAPTER VIII

Lighting Your Stage

LET us imagine that we are seated in a dimly lighted theater. The signal rings. The curtains open and what do we see? People. What makes them visible? Light. What makes the color? Light. What makes the interesting shadows? Light. It is light that does all these things, makes the picture visible and carries our thoughts and feelings into the play which is about to begin.

By what means is all this done? By means of footlights, overhead lights, movable strips of lights, and movable spotlights. A few years ago every stage was lighted by footlights only. These lights threw a crude glare on to the faces of the actors and sometimes made large ugly shadows on the back drop. Later, when overhead lights were used with footlights, there were no shadows at all. This was equally bad. The majority of people did not seem to mind this, but when certain artists went to the theater, they began to ask themselves whether there might not be some way of remedying the glare of the footlights and of managing the shadows. These artists began to experiment. They made little stages, took the footlights away, and began, by means of arc lights, to light their stages indirectly. They began to use movable spot-lights behind the scenes, and to fasten lights on to strips of wood and place these strips wherever they felt they were necessary.

They made further experiments. They covered their lights with pieces of different colored silks and gelatine. This not only removed the glare of the lights but produced new and very interesting effects. Next they turned to Nature and began to observe how she produced her wonderful effects. They discovered that these usually came in the soft light of early morning and late evening, in twilight and moonlight, and not in the strong garish light of mid-day. With these observations in mind, they went to work to re-produce some of these effects. The result of their experiments is that, to-day, we see stage pictures as beautiful as pictures painted by the finest artists. Lighting has now come to be such an important factor in the producing of plays that no stage, however small, can ignore it.

Let us now consider the kind of lighting which may be used in the several kinds of marionette stages. The Punch and Judy stage requires no lighting when used in daylight. But even this stage requires some thought for its lighting when it is used in a darkened room. Your set of Christmas-tree lights may be fastened to the top of the proscenium arch and an extension light may be used in the same way as is shown in the illustration. Christmas-tree lights and extension lights are all that are necessary for the table stage and the soap-box stage. In the chapter on "Making Your Stage" you will see how these lights are placed.

If you have made the semi-professional stage with overhead lights, footlights, and strips, you are ready to experiment with your lighting. Begin by asking yourself whether the scenes of your play take place indoors or out of doors. What is the time of day and the season of the year? Is it an out-of-door scene, representing the cold of winter, or the heat of summer? Does your scene occur in the soft light of early morning or in the glow of sunset? Is your scene laid in a deep cool wood or in a warm sunny garden? All of these questions must be considered.

Now, how can you produce these varied effects of sunlight and moonlight, coldness and warmth, somberness and gaiety? Certain colors such as red, orange, and yellow are called warm colors, because they give the feeling of warmth. Other colors such as green, blue, and violet are called cool, because they give the feeling of coolness. If your scene suggests warmth, whether indoors or out of doors, begin experimenting with warm lights, ambers, reds, and yellows. You will find that usually a certain number of white lights are needed with the colored lights in order to produce the effects you seek.

Everyone knows that color produces varied emotions. We are familiar with the effects of red which

Marionette Ballet, "Petrouchka"

are stimulating, exciting, or irritating. The toreador, recognizing this principle, waves a flaming red mantle before the bull. Blue has an exactly opposite effect. It quiets and soothes, and when it runs into violet, it becomes depressing. Experiment with purple lights and you will find that they give a note of gloom, mystery, or of impending disaster. Yellow is the color that brings gaiety and light-heartedness, as you will recall when you contrast your own feelings on a sunshiny day and on a gray day.

You will find that most out-of-door effects are produced by soft natural lighting which gives a sense of distance and perspective to the scene. For this effect use yellow, amber, and white lights with an occasional blue or red. Only lights coming from several directions will produce the subtle tones of nature. This means using footlights with discretion, stronger lights overhead, and placing strips wherever you need them in order to destroy the shadows which other lights may throw. Sometimes it takes several hours of experimenting to find the right lighting for a single scene. It means changing the position of the strips, using more lighting or less lighting, and always asking yourself whether your lighting is just that which your scene demands to bring out its mood. The shadows produced by footlights may sometimes be used to give charm or mystery to a scene. For instance, in the second scene in the *Petrouchka Ballet,* only footlights were used. The pattern of the shadows of the dancers falling on a neutral background was very effective.

If your scene is laid indoors, your lighting will be

somewhat determined by the period of the play. For instance, in the third act of *Men of Iron*, the great hall of Devlen Castle was softly lighted to suggest candle and torch light. This effect was produced by using amber and blue lights overhead; red, blue, white, and amber in the footlights. A strip of blue and red lights placed upright against the proscenium frame threw rich color against the king and those of his courtiers who stood near the throne. This color was most pleasing when it fell upon the armor of Myles as he knelt before the king.

ᵂ Again your lighting may be determined by the kind of action. A gay scene naturally requires bright lighting. As an illustration of this: The royal kitchen in the *Knave of Hearts* was made warm and gay by the use of white and amber lights overhead, and amber, blue, and red footlights to throw rich colors on the costumes. The fireplace gave a warm light, and through the window could be seen the bright summer landscape.

As an illustration of a serious and somber scene, we might take the first act of the hero tale, *Sigurd, the Volsung*, Here many blue lights were used with a very few red and amber. The result was that the great hall became a mysterious place in which Odin himself could appear, and a somber enough setting for the traitorous Siggeir.

If your picture is an imaginative one, such as the garden of jewels in *Aladdin and His Wonderful Lamp*, you are free to use your lights as you wish, to produce a scene of enchantment.

When you have finished your experimenting, and have found the right lighting for a scene, take a sheet of paper and make a chart. This illustration suggests a form for you to follow.

CHART

Name of Play

Scene I.

Overhead lights.

Left (as seen from the audience)   Right

blue, white, white, white, blue

Footlights

Left   Right

blue, red, amber, white, red, blue

Left strip

blue, red, blue, blue

                                           Right strip

blue, amber, blue, blue

Left extension

white

The stage electrician will need a chart for each scene of your play. The changing of the lights for each scene will be his responsibility.

You will probably have little need for baby-spots unless your equipment is very elaborate, and to use them requires almost professional experience. Every boy who is interested in electricity knows that a rheostat or dimmer is used for turning lights off and on gradually. They may be purchased for a small sum or they may be made.

Every new play and every new scene presents a new problem for you to solve. You will know that you have solved your problem when, as a group, you can

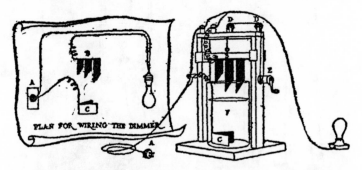

From A the current from one wire passes to the stationary electrode C which is submerged in a gallon jar of water containing one eighth teaspoon of ammonium chloride. The graduated electrodes (all connected) are fastened to the wooden bar B which is made to slide up and down the vertical posts at either side. Both sets of electrodes are made of thin sheet copper. By means of the cord (attached to the screw eye in B) which runs over the pulleys D, D down to the spool drum E, the upper electrodes can be slowly let down into the ammonium chloride solution, completing the circuit and increasing it as more of the electrode surface is exposed to the liquid. This dimmer will carry as many lights as your theater will ever require.

sit before each scene and feel that it is harmonious, that it surrounds the figures with suitable atmosphere, and that your lighting interprets the idea and mood of your play.

CHAPTER IX

Training Your Puppeteers

THE stage is set. The play has been chosen. The puppets are ready. Let us gather around the table to talk about our parts. There should be a copy of the play in the hands of each puppeteer. Begin by reading the play, each pupil reading the part that he has chosen. After the reading, discuss and analyze each character, his appearance, his disposition, and his voice.

For instance, Captain Peggotty in *The Childhood of David Copperfield* would have a rough-and-ready seaman's voice that would boom from his deep chest, but his words would show generosity and kindness. Alice, in *Alice in Wonderland* would have a little girl's voice, one that would suggest wonderment, sometimes impatience, and a quaint dignity when she tried to appear grown up. The White Rabbit's voice would be high, nervous, and impatient. The Caterpillar would have a slow, full, dignified voice, while the voice of the Duchess would be gruff and peppery. Diccon Bowman, the faithful old servant in *Men of Iron*, would have the trembling, wavering voice of extreme old age.

How shall the right person be found for each part? One of the most satisfactory ways is that of trying out for parts, with the group acting as a jury. The judges must keep in mind that the voice is very important in interpreting character and they will do well to choose the voice that is best suited to the character. If each puppeteer takes the same position at the table at each rehearsal, you will soon associate each voice with a certain place. This will make it much easier to address your lines to the proper character. The lines should be reread slowly for the sake of better understanding. In this way, each in turn soon comes to read the lines of his character with real appreciation. Do not hurry over the little words. Every word should be clearly spoken. Lift your eyes as often as you can from your manuscript. "Talk" your lines. In almost no time you will know your lines without looking at them. When you can speak your lines so naturally that any of your friends, with his eyes closed, could imagine the character you are interpreting from your voice, you are ready to take your puppet in hand.

Manipulation of your marionette is the second step in your training as a puppeteer. You will be surprised at the amount of time this requires. Some of the great-

est puppeteers have spent months learning to manage a single puppet. In all your practice work, avoid careless motions of your hands, with your thoughts elsewhere. Be wholly absorbed in what you wish to do.

Your puppet in the making has been so weighted that when you hold your controller you will know the very second the puppet's feet touch the floor. This delicate position must be held. Hold your controller steady. If you lower your controller after the feet have touched the floor your puppet will sag. Be-

hold the sagging puppet! Begin gently. Do not jerk the strings. The least motion of the hand brings a quick response from the puppet. In fact, puppets are just like ourselves, if handled skilfully they will do almost anything you may wish them to do. As your skill grows so will your pleasure in your puppet grow. Its many almost human movements and gestures will delight you as they have delighted all those men and women who have been its friends. If you can hold your marionette before a mirror and practise with it, speaking your lines, as you pull the strings, you will be surprised to see how lifelike it becomes. You will discover that a slight movement may indicate very strong feeling.

A whole chapter could be written about the movements of the head. Let us see how the head may show thoughtfulness. When you are thoughtful, how do you hold your head? Release the head strings and your puppet's head will drop forward as yours has just done. If you wish to turn this thoughtful pose into one of discouragement, let the shoulders droop forward as well, so that the chest becomes hollow. How would you stand if listening? Release the head strings and slant the controller so that the head falls a little to one side and a little forward. How near to this and yet how different is the attitude of craftiness and cunning. To the listening pose you simply add a forward thrust of the head and a hunching up of the shoulders. For the proud, erect bearing of a king, hold your controller horizontally. If your puppet is a charming young lady, her head will make many quick, graceful little turns. This may be done by releasing the head strings and tipping the controller back and forth.

We now come to the movements of the shoulders and the waist. The center string controls the movements of the waist and is used whenever you want your puppet to sit down, kneel down, or bow. As you know there are a hundred different ways of sitting down. The young and old, each has his way. So, too, have the proud and the humble, the gentle and the boisterous. When you make your puppet sit down, unless he is very stiff and proud, let his body settle a little. You will notice that most people do this. When you pull the center string you must at the same time lower the controller slightly to keep the feet from swinging off the floor.

There are quite as many ways of bowing as there are of sitting down. A courtier would bow from the waist, his head slightly bent; the little princess, in her full skirts, would courtesy gracefully with her head tilted backward.

Next, we come to that small but important thing, the hand. When one knows how to control it, it can do such wonderful things. It can show force or gentleness, harshness or kindness, nervous excitement or shaky old age. It is possible for a marionette to draw a sword, practise at the pells, engage in fist fights, and hammer at a forge. When a marionette must hammer at a forge, as in *Sigurd, the Volsung,* and in *Men of Iron,* be sure that it makes a heavy, steady stroke. The hammer must be of iron. If the armorer sings a jolly rhythmic song, he can keep time with his hammer. Suit your gestures to your words. It is the fault of inexperienced puppeteers that they make all gestures alike. Experienced puppeteers suit their gestures to the ideas and to the feelings which they wish to convey.

It is when a puppet is called upon to do some unusual thing, such as dancing, climbing a wall, fighting a duel, riding a horse in a tournament, that difficulties appear.

Let us take the first of these—dancing. The Bear in *Men of Iron* danced. Dainty little Lady Alice in *Men of Iron* danced. Fat jolly Tweedle Dee in *Alice in Wonderland* danced. The surly old cook in the Duchess's kitchen danced. But imagine the differences in these dances! Each dance expressed the character of the dancer. The Bear danced to a lively jig whistled by his trainer. His steps were carefully worked out in time with the tune, and when once learned were never varied. Little Lady Alice, with dainty step and charming courtesies, danced to the tune of a medieval love song. Tweedle Dee danced to a rollicking tune played on an accordion. His steps were lively and when he danced across the stage on his right foot, kicking out his left in time with the music, he made everyone laugh. The cook's dance was an Irish jig.

Puppets are versatile. To them belongs not only the interpretation of the spoken word but they are equally at home in the world of pantomime, music, and dance.

The illustrations in this book show how puppets can even perform a ballet. Here you can see their interpretation of the colorful and dramatic Russian ballet, *Petrouchka*. The cast of twenty-one puppets included four principal actors, the manager, the Moor, the Ballerina, and Petrouchka and besides these, a showman and a trained bear, an organ grinder, and bands of gypsies.

A ballet or an opera will naturally require a different procedure than a play, because the character analysis comes from the music. Here are the steps by which the *Petrouchka Ballet* was worked out:

1. The story was told to the pupils.

2. The musical score as a whole was played to them.

3. The motif for each character and incident was played to them.

4. The musical score as a whole was again played and the pupils listened for the motifs.

5. Each character was analyzed and his probable actions upon the stage were discussed.

6. The puppet was taken in hand and the interpretation of the music with it was begun.

There are four scenes in this ballet. The first scene is a street fair in a Russian village. A little theater occupies the center back stage in which the stage manager exhibits the Moor, the Ballerina, and Petrouchka. The scene closes with their lively dance and Petrouchka's declaration of love to the Ballerina.

Scene II is in Petrouchka's box and shows his despairing love for the Ballerina.

Scene III is in the Moor's box and shows him playing with his ball. The Ballerina enters and they dance together. Petrouchka rushes in and in a jealous rage tries to kill the Moor. The Moor chases Petrouchka out of his box.

Scene IV is again at the fair. There are gay dances by gypsies and nounous. Petrouchka runs in, chased by the Moor who stabs him. The people draw away and the Ballerina kneels beside him. The manager comes in, the Moor, the Ballerina, and all the people depart. The manager drags poor, lifeless Petrouchka toward the little theater. Suddenly up over the little theater appears the spirit of Petrouchka, mocking and gesticulating. The manager stands aghast.

So that you may understand how this ballet was produced, let us take the second scene and work it out together. The scene opens with a crashing chord as Petrouchka is thrown onto the stage. (No less than thirty times did the puppeteer rehearse this entrance with the music.) He lay in a motionless heap. At a few plaintive notes he lifts his head, then drops it again. To the quick notes that follow he beats the floor with his hands. As the music grows in volume, his despair increases, and he leaps to his feet and rushes wildly about the room, beating frantically upon the walls. As the music changes and becomes soft and rer 'niscent, Petrouchka thinks of the Ballerina and stretches out his arms, then sorrowfully drops his head. The motif for the Ballerina announces her entrance. She comes in gay and light as a bird. Petrouchka, overcome with emotion, drops on his knees before her. She continues her gay little dance and leaves as lightly as she entered. Despair again seizes Petrouchka, who dashes himself against the walls, then finally falls to the ground. The curtains close.

In a gymnasium there are certain exercises that bring all the muscles of the body into use. Likewise there are times when the whole body of a marionette must come into action. If you want a marionette to climb a wall, your audience must feel that the marionette is actually pulling himself, with effort, up and over the wall. This requires a great deal of patient practice. To make your marionette climb a wall, he must first appear to catch hold of the wall, then to draw up one knee, then to strain up as you would, then to throw an arm over the wall, then to pull his body up until he can throw a leg over the wall. If this is well done, the audience climbs the walls with the puppet.

Sometimes, puppets must appear to assist each other. For instance, when Myles was thrown on the ground by the bully, Walter Blunt, Gascoyne, his friend, got down on one knee beside him, threw his arm around his shoulders, and apparently helped him to rise.

There are certain little tricks which are very effective, such as crying, or dropping off to sleep and snoring. In the *Childhood of David Copperfield*, Mrs. Gummidge frequently lifted her apron to her eyes and wept. As one corner of her apron was sewed to her hand, this was an easy thing to do. Can you see her, shoulders shaking, her apron to her eyes, sniffling, "I am a lone, lorn critter and everything goes contrary with me?"

Perhaps you might like to know how a puppet may appear to toss a ball. This is the way it was done. One puppeteer held the Moor's controller while his assistant held the end of a string attached to the ball. Through practice, these puppeteers were able to make the Moor's hand and the ball rise at the same moment, thereby giving the impression that the Moor tossed the ball. When the Moor stopped playing with the ball, the puppeteer who held the string attached to the ball let it fall to the stage. The audience felt that the Moor was tired of playing and had tossed the ball aside.

In this same ballet, an organ grinder appeared. The handle of the organ was fastened to one of his hands. When the puppeteer pulled the hand string up and down in time with the music, it seemed to the audience that the organ was really being played. A marionette can be made to play a flute. The flute is fastened in one hand, and a string from the flute passed through the mouth of the marionette up through the top of its head to the controller. When the puppeteer pulls the flute string, the flute is raised to the mouth of the marionette.

All these effects and many others can be accomplished when you understand the manipulation of your strings. Sometimes you may wish to use birds, bees, butterflies, or flying dragons. If you keep the wings in constant motion you can make your audience believe that these winged creatures are really flying. Of course, bees and butterflies move their wings more rapidly than birds and dragons. The more you observe flying birds, the better you will be able to imitate them.

You have made the puppet look the part, now see that it acts the part. You have made your hero look like a hero, now see that he acts like a hero. You made the king look like a king. Can you make him act like a king?

The third step in your training as a puppeteer comes when you have acquired enough skill to manage your puppet. Then you are ready to join your fellow puppeteers on the bridge. At first you will probably feel that the bridge is not large enough for you alone, not to mention four or five others. Experience will show you, however, that you can do a great deal in a very small space. This means good management and practice and consideration for your fellow puppeteers.

Now that the puppet is on the stage, imagine what a shock it would be to your audience to see a great hand coming down below the proscenium arch. To prevent this, always keep your hand, even during rehearsals, close to your control.

While on the stage, every motion must have a reason behind it. Puppets cannot move aimlessly about the stage any more than real actors can. Every gesture, too, must mean something.

Now the time has come to show yourselves as real artists. Your stage is your picture and though you change it with every move of your puppets, you are always making it the picture. This means that you should know what artists speak of as arrangement or composition.

Let us suppose that you are sitting in the audience and saw two puppets standing like this: "Oh,

how stupid," you would say. Imagine them standing like this:

"How interesting." But why interesting? The first spacing was equal, hence it was monotonous. The

Upper: Marionettes from "The Adventures of Alice."
Lower Left: Bear and Trainer from "Men of Iron."
Lower Right: Marionette from "Petrouchka"

second was varied, therefore, more interesting. Again you are sitting in the audience looking at the picture and this is what you see:

Two small figures on one side and one large figure on the other side. How satisfying! The reason is balance. You can see by these two simple illustrations how necessary it is to keep in mind not only the movements of your puppets, but the positions of all the puppets on the stage. If each puppeteer understands this and considers the relation of his puppet to every other puppet, the audience will always see an interesting picture.

Equally as important as the stage picture is the conduct of your puppets when on the stage. They should all show interest when another puppet is speaking. This may be done by turning the head to listen, nodding the head to show agreement, shaking the head to show disagreement, leaning forward to show interest. In a hundred small ways a puppet can show life. The point is, there should be no dead puppets on the stage.

But there is a danger here. Puppets must not divert the attention of the audience from the main character. For example, in *Men of Iron* in the scene showing the great hall of Devlen Castle, the minstrel is singing before the king and his court. The jester, with his pranks and capers, could easily have taken too much of the attention of the audience to himself and away from the minstrel, but instead, he sat down on the floor near the minstrel and pretended to be playing a lute. He followed every gesture of the minstrel and when the minstrel finished his song, rose and bowed low before the king. The jester did likewise, to the amusement of the audience.

Good puppeteering is much like good ball playing, the interest is in the ball but the ball always moves. It goes from player to player. Any player who holds the ball is the center of interest, some longer and some shorter. Your skill and cleverness can keep this sense of movement and interest in your puppets and their play. This smoothness is accomplished by your quickness in watching for the last words spoken by the speaker before you, which is called your cue; and also by your cleverness in planning ways to help out a puppeteer and his puppet who has difficult things to do.

When the bear trainer, for example, commands his bear to stand on his head, the boy who is holding the bear's controller must have time enough to make the difficult manipulation of the strings. If the puppeteers who manage the squires make their puppets lean forward and call out in surprise to each other, "What? A trick?" "The bear can do a trick." "Look."

"Bravo!" "Bravo!" (as the bear succeeds in standing on its head), they will be of great assistance to the bear puppeteer.

Here is an illustration of the way in which you can avoid awkward pauses. The Knave of Hearts, in the play by that name, steals some tarts and climbs out of the window. Now you can see that his puppeteer would need plenty of time in getting the knave through the window. Lady Violetta, who helps him steal the tarts, shows great excitement and cries to him to hurry, then she runs to the door, saying that she hears someone coming. Then she runs back again. She repeats this until the knave has made his escape. You can easily imagine how this clever trick excited the audience.

Getting your puppet off the stage is just as important as getting it on. Time your exits so that there is no awkward pause between the last word spoken and the exit.

You have imagined yourself sitting in the audience seeing a picture. Now can you imagine your disappointment when you cannot understand a single word the puppets say? Inexperienced puppeteers are apt to think that it is the high, loud voice that will reach the people in the last row of seats. Experienced puppeteers know that it is the clear, full, rich voice that carries. Address your words to those farthest away from you. Keep in mind that your voice must travel down and out through the proscenium arch. If your head is not lowered, your voice will strike the curtain, which will deaden it.

Sometimes it is necessary to make the voice seem to come from a distance and yet every word must be distinct. This can be done in a very simple way. Bend your arm and lift it to your face, holding your mouth inside your elbow. Now when you speak, your words seem to come from a distance. As you slowly lift your mouth from your arm, your voice seems to come nearer and nearer. In *Sigurd, the Volsung*, there is a scene where the dragon, who possesses a treasure of gold, comes, at twilight, out of the rocky crevice of a great cliff, to drink at a pool. Before he is seen, his voice is dimly heard calling, "Gold, gold, my gold, my gold." The boy who spoke these lines used this trick so cleverly that his audience shivered as the dragon appeared.

Every person knows that the greatest charm of a voice is its naturalness. This naturalness comes to you when you let your feelings go down the strings into your puppet. Then it is that your puppet comes to life, is gay, sad, prankish, haughty, timid, bold, willful, cunning, sly, or lovable. When your puppet obeys your every feeling, you and your puppet are one.

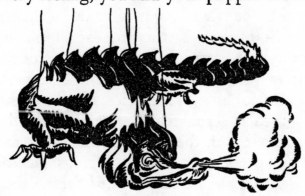

CHAPTER X

Presenting Your Play

THE successful presenting of a play requires much planning and organization. It will be necessary to choose a property man, two assistants, a stage electrician, an inspector of the strings, one assistant, and a prompter. It is the business of the property man to see that the scenery and properties are in perfect condition before each performance. He, with his assistant, sets the stage long in advance of the performance. He changes the settings for each act. It is necessary for him to have two assistants, one for the right and one for the left of the stage. The property man finds places for all his properties. He places the properties for each scene together. He places the back drops and wings in the order in which they are to be used. Each property, when not in use, should be in its place. Benches should be provided behind the scenes for the puppeteers. If chairs are used, beware of squeaky ones.

The stage electrician is responsible for the lights and the making of all changes in lighting between acts. He must be provided with a chart of instructions, giving the lighting plan for every scene. This plan should be securely tacked where it can be easily referred to. The electrician can also take care of the drawing of the curtains, which is an important task. There should also be a sheet of cues for the drawing of the curtains, since a scene can be spoiled by drawing the curtains too soon, too quickly, too slowly, or too jerkily. The last words spoken in the first scene of *Men of Iron* were: "I will climb the wall and fetch it." This was the signal or cue for the electrician to close the curtains.

The prompter ought to have a low, clear voice and ought to be a person in whom every puppeteer has confidence. Girls usually make good prompters because of the quality of their voices. The prompter should stand on the bridge near the middle and always keep her eyes on the lines. She should never fail to prompt a puppeteer the instant he needs it. She never confuses the puppeteers by trying to prompt them when they do not need it. She must know the play so well that she understands every pause.

The inspector of the strings is another important person in the organization. This office is usually well filled by a girl. If there are a great many puppets she may need an assistant. It is her duty to test all the strings about a half hour before the play. This is done by placing the thumb and forefinger on the string, just under the controller, then letting the string pass between the thumb and forefinger as they travel down to the marionette. If there is a weak part in the string it can be easily detected. She sees that the fastening at the controller is secure, and that the strings hang straight and untangled from the controller to the marionette. She should provide a first-aid box fully equipped with scissors, thread, paper of pins, thumb tacks, and needles. A threaded needle, with the thread the length of the knee strings, can be pinned into the curtain so that it is available the second it is needed. A place for everything, and everything in its place, does much toward making your performance move along with smoothness and rapidity. All puppeteers, including property man, electrician, and prompter should wear gymnasium shoes. In fact, anyone who assists behind the scenes should do the same. If you find that your bridge stairs creak the puppeteers should remain on the bridge throughout the scene. Before a puppeteer comes down from the bridge, he hangs up his marionette.

Since silence is so necessary behind the scenes, it can readily be understood how important it is to have absolutely no talking on the bridge, or between puppeteers who are waiting behind the stage. Scenes must be changed and properties moved almost noiselessly. If you have a high ideal of perfection for your play, two or three weeks of daily rehearsals will be necessary. This is especially true for any marionette ballet, such as Petrouchka, where it is necessary to memorize the music, because each puppeteer is dependent on the music for his cues. Before the curtains open all marionettes that are to be in the scene should be in their places on the stage. Hold your controller with a steady hand, so that your marionette is motionless. Keep your puppet on its feet. Do not let it sag. Remember the sagging puppet.

As soon as the curtains open, begin your lines. Remember that a play is like a piece of music, it moves onward in perfect time. An awkward pause, or hesitation, breaks the time and destroys the spell you are weaving about your audience. Entrances and exits should be so arranged that the marionette makes his entrance and begins to speak his lines as soon as the speaker before him finishes his lines. We have spoken of the spell that you are trying to weave. Let us see what has been done, so far, toward this end. The puppets are beautifully made. The scenery is lovely in design and color. Hands, through patient practice, have acquired that deftness and sureness that we call skill. The voices are well pitched and appropriate for each character.

The greatest thing, however, is yet to be done. It is to touch the imagination of your audience. The key to this world of the imagination is suggestion. The lights and setting give the mood. The voices and the movements of the puppets convey the thoughts and emotions of the characters of the play. The harmony of lights, setting, voices, and the movements of the puppets work the spell.

In the battle scene in *Sigurd, the Volsung,* the

curtains open on a stage where a low mound and one tree is silhouetted against a twilight sky. A bit of afterglow still lingers. On the ground are several shields and spears and two prostrate figures. Against one of the figures lies Sigmund, the great Norse hero. Beside him kneels his faithful wife, Hiordis. The audience feels that, shrouded in the mysterious blue light, are a great host of noble slain. Sigmund bids Hiordis gather up the pieces of his broken sword to keep for his son that is to be born. Out of the shadows, dimly seen in his "gleaming gray mantle and cloud-blue hood," comes Odin, to welcome Sigmund to the hall of the heroes in Walhalla. Hiordis bows her head in silence and the audience experiences her grief, and shares her hope for the future. The afterglow in the sky seems to be a promise of a new day.

MASKS

CHAPTER I

The Map of the Mask

FROM the map it is evident that masks have been worn in every part of the world. They are older than the idols which primitive man made for himself. Why he invented masks we do not exactly know. They may have originated when man first attempted to impersonate the gods as he sought to control nature. If you can imagine how vast and mysterious the world of nature looked to primitive man and how he felt about all moving things, animals, clouds, winds, flowing water, swaying trees, and creeping vines, you can understand how he came to believe that there were spirits dwelling in such things and that these indwelling spirits had power to work him good or evil. Through offerings and prayers he sought to control these mysterious spirits and make them do his will.

Death was the greatest of all mysteries. Where did the spirit go when it left the body? It must go somewhere. Why not into an animal, or a tree, or even into a stone? Gradually this came to be his belief. His desire for mastery and power over the spirits led him to imagine faces more powerful and compelling than his own which would dominate them. He was full of invention. He invented the mask and became a god. When he wore the mask he believed that he controlled indwelling spirits and even coming events. This belief was true of primitive man the world over.

In Africa, masks were always worn in the tribal religious rites. When a dancer wore a mask, he was no longer an individual for he felt within himself the spirit of all his tribe. When the dance was finished, the mask was taken from the head and worshiped like an idol. These masks were created by the greatest artists of the tribe. They were simple, strong, and severe, without naturalism of any kind. They exaggerated the character of eyes, nose, and mouth in order to give intensity of expression. They were strange, but not terrifying. They were an effort to reveal the inner relations of man, nature, and God. They were beautifully made out of wood, copper, bronze, and ivory.

Quite different masks are found among the primitive people of North America. The Eskimos in Alaska make animal masks such as of the bear, wolf, beaver, and various birds to represent their totem ancestors. Every totemistic tribe has its own animal ancestor which it believes is impressed upon everything around the dwelling. The Eskimos believe that in the early days, if animals wished to assume human form, they could do so at will by pushing up their faces or beaks, as if they were masks. This human or man-like form they called the "inua." It was supposed to represent the thinking part of the animal, and, at its death, became its shade or ghost. During the many festivals when the Eskimos wore their animal masks, they believed that they actually became the creature that they represented. Some of their masks were ingeniously made with double faces, so arranged that, at certain times in the ceremony, the outer mask which was held in place by pegs could be removed, thus symbolizing the transformation of the animal into the man.

The Indians of California observe annual ceremonies of mourning for the dead. Ten or more men prepare themselves to play the part of the ghosts. Disguised with painted masks, and adorned with feathers and grasses, they dance and sing in the village or rush about at night in the forest, with burning torches in their hands. The relatives of the dead look upon the maskers as their departed friends.

Other Indian tribes disguise themselves by painting their faces instead of wearing masks. The inspiration for the painting comes from a trance or a vision. The dancer makes his request to the leader of the ceremony. "My Father, I have come to be painted, so that I may see my friends. Have pity on me and paint me." Elaborate designs in red, yellow, green, and blue are put upon the face, with a red or yellow line upon the parting of the hair. The designs most commonly used are sun, moon, stars, crosses, and birds.

The Indians of Arizona and New Mexico, such as

the Hopi and Zuni, are ancestor worshipers. They believe that their dead relatives become supernatural spirits or "cachinas" or "kokos." They consider them guardians that they may call upon in time of distress and need. If the crops have suffered from drought, they bring out the sacred masks and perform the rain dance.

The Zuni believe that the earth is watered by these departed ancestors, who as they pass to and fro continuously over the middle plains collect water in vases and gourd jugs from the six great waters of the world. They are unseen by the people below, because they wear cloud masks.

The masks worn by the Zuni dancers in their great winter festivals bear symbols characteristic of the cachinas and are repainted with great care before each dance. Many and varied are the names of the different masks, such as Mountain Goat-hunter Mask, Thrush Mask, Owl Mask, Buffalo Mask, Dust-in-the-House Woman Mask, Rain-Drop-Maker Mask, Long-Life-Maker Mask.

The ancient Aztecs wore masks decorated with turquoise and shell.

In Brazil, masks were used in dances performed in honor of the dead. The mask represented animals, birds, and insects. They obtained their magical power by the wearer imitating the movements and actions of these creatures. For instance, the butterfly masks came by their magic through the dance of two men who imitated the play of these brilliant insects fluttering on the wing, settling on sand banks and rocks.

Masks made by students in Summer School, Cleveland School of Education

Indian Corn Maidens
Clowns
Japanese Characters: Old Woman, Devil Mask, Old Man

The magic of the swallow masks came through the imitation of the swallow, and so it was with the owl, spider, vulture, beetle, toad, jaguar mask, and others. After the dance the masks were burned in order to drive the indwelling spirits back to their haunts. Even idols needed masks to give them life, and special power over disease and disaster. These masks must be as enduring as the gods themselves, so they were made of terra cotta, shell, and stone. Among the gifts made to Columbus when he landed in San Salvador were some of these sacred masks.

Masks originated in Asia just as they did in Africa and America, through man's fears and superstitions. In India, China, Japan, and throughout the Orient, they have been used for centuries in religious cere-monies. Gradually they were introduced into court functions, such as wedding and birthday celebrations, and finally animal masks were used to entertain the common people.

The highly involved religions of these eastern peoples, with their countless deities, brought infinite variety to their masks. Their civilization, being old and rich in tradition, gave to the mask subtelties and refinement of characterization that could not be con-ceived of by primitive peoples. Their masks reflected their clear, well-defined ideas, and showed their ar-tists' amazing ability to recognize and analyze expres-sions of the human face. Tranquillity, mirth, cunning, scorn, wrath, and subtle shades of feeling are por-trayed. The idea in the mind of the mask maker was so clear that we are never left in doubt as to the meaning of the mask. They are emotional interpretations, never realistic portraits.

Chinese priests used the mask in morality plays showing the rewards and punishments that will be meted out in their many heavens, hells, and purgatories. Their masks are usually horrible or terrifying, sometimes humorous, rarely beautiful. They are worn by gorgeously costumed priests who enact the plays, in pantomime, on stages erected in the temple courtyards.

In Siam, Burma, Java, and Ceylon, the mask passed from the temple to the theater and the strolling players. Much of its old symbolism has been lost, and it frequently becomes merely an elaborate piece of decoration.

Probably the most beautiful masks in the world are the religious or *No* masks of Japan. These are worn in the sacred *No* plays, of which there are more than two hundred. They represent the Japanese idea of the appearance of their gods and heroes. Music, dance, and dialogue all are used in the five or six short plays which make the *No* cycle. The *No* begins with the bestowing of blessings by the gods and their victory over the demons. A short love story follows, with possibly a bit of humor, and then a picture of the passing of life. The end is a gracious recognition of the favor of the gods. These ancient plays are performed out of doors on a simple platform erected against a wall on which is painted a symbolic pine tree. Masks have been used for more than four hundred years in these *No* dramas.

The ancient Egyptians used the mask in their sacrificial ceremonies. In the "Book of the Dead" ceremony one may see a priest wearing the jackal-headed mask of Anubis, standing before the bier of the great god, Osiris. The victims kneeling before him wear hare and hawk headed masks. Egyptian kings wore lion, bull, and dragon masks to impress their subjects with their mighty power. Even the mummies wore masks. On the faces of their dead kings they placed masks of pure gold as did the Mycenæans.

The mask, as we know it, came to us through the Greeks. In the worship of Demeter, the earth mother of the Greeks, masks of horses, pigs, cats, hares, and asses were used. Masks were also used in the worship of Dionysus, with dancing, chanting, and chorus. The Greeks, being the first people to have a theater, were also the first people to realize that no human face could portray the sustained expression of tragedy and comedy called for by the great rôles of their dramas. The mask became a necessity. Thespis is credited with its invention. The mask enabled an actor to play female rôles, to play many different characters, and to represent his character in youth, middle life, and old age. The open mouth characterized the Greek mask. Some scholars have believed that a brass mouthpiece was used to amplify the voice of the actor.

The Romans appropriated the Greek mask. Virgil tells us that they hung masks on trees at the time of sowing, in order to better the crops. Noble Romans wore masks of their illustrious ancestors at funerals. The impersonators riding in chariots through the streets were dressed in rich robes of office, resplendent in purple and gold such as the dead nobles had worn in their lifetime. When the funeral procession reached the Forum, the maskers solemnly took their seats on the ivory chairs placed for them on the platform of the rostra, in the sight of all the people. This spectacle, no doubt, stirred memories of the glorious past in the hearts of the old and fired the young with noble ambitions. It is said that Nero wore masks resembling his own face and those of his favorites.

With the passing of glorious Rome the mask became a degraded thing, abhorred by the early Christians.

Throughout the Dark Ages in Europe the mask was used only in the revels, and to celebrate the coming of the New Year and the springtime. Gradually the spirit of revelling slipped into the Church. In England and in France, during the XIIth Century, there was a very famous revel called "The Feast of Fools" that began at vespers on the last day of the year. Two equally famous revels were those of the "Boy Bishop" and the "Feast of the Ass," celebrated with rout and mock ritual. Such were the excesses indulged in that Pope Innocent III, in 1207 A. D., formally prohibited masking in the church. But it was not until the XVth Century that these revels were effectively driven out. We hear next of the mask in scriptural plays, such as those given at Christmas time. These plays were performed outside the church. During the XIVth Century, we discover the guilds or corporations of craftsmen employing the mask in their religious plays, in honor of royal visits, and in their May Day processions. In fact, all over Europe, at that time wherever

Masks
Upper Row: *Bishop, Queen, King*
Middle Row: *Lady-in-Waiting, Crusader, Child*
Lower Row: *Jester, Old Woman, Little Jack*

the mystery, miracle, or morality play was given, we are sure to find at least occasional use of the mask.

In Italy, from the XIVth to the XVIIth Century, the mask was worn by Harlequin, Pantaloon, Pulcinella, the Doctor, and all the characters of the *Commedia dell 'arte*. In the XVIIIth Century, the comedy theaters of France also affected the mask as a dramatic requisite.

During the XIXth Century the mask had degenerated to the crude false faces used by Europeans or their descendants in America. In Philadelphia, children wear masks at Thanksgiving. Masks appear at the celebration of the Mardi Gras in New Orleans, and the old-time custom of wearing masks at Hallowe'en still prevails.

A few years ago a group of artists, foremost among them W. T. Benda, who knew the great and beautiful tradition of the mask and had felt its strange fascination, lifted the mask to a new level of distinction. Anyone who has had the good fortune to see one of their masks cannot escape its spell nor can he rest until he finds an occasion to make a mask.

CHAPTER II

Occasions for Wearing the Mask

WE ALL know the thrill of wearing a mask, but an entirely new and strange thrill awaits him who wears a mask of his own creation. Anyone who has imagination is apt to turn away from the ordinary commercial mask, because his fancy can picture something much more clever and interesting.

When one looks at the calendar he is surprised to find that there are so many days that invite the wearing of masks. The first occasion for wearing a mask that comes to mind is Hallowe'en, that old celebration of the eve of All Saints' Day. The religious significance of this festival is almost forgotten, but it still marks the fullness of the harvest time and has long been celebrated with masks and merry-making. Even the glowing jack-o'-lantern is a kind of mask.

For occasions such as the New Year and April Fools' Day the mask may express an individual idea or fancy. There are a few days, however, such as Thanksgiving, Christmas, and Easter, for which masks must be specially designed. These masks should represent the characters that one associates with the occasions. When a story is woven about these characters and then told in pantomime, by actors wearing masks, it may be called a mask. Music and dance add much to the beauty of a mask.

Woodland, park, and garden are ideal settings for masks in spring, summer, and autumn. Arbor Day, Shakespeare's birthday, and May Day are delightful occasions which stir the imagination and have rich associations in music and literature.

Let us suppose that one wishes to celebrate Christmas with a mask. Christmas is a Christian festival but it is being celebrated more and more by all people who believe in brotherly love and good will. These attributes can become the theme of the mask. The possibilities for developing this theme of brotherly love and good will are endless. The story may be laid in any land. It may center about the life of a great court or about the humblest home. But wherever it is laid, the story must have dramatic interest and touch the feelings of those who see it.

A simple mask may be just as beautiful and moving as a very elaborate mask. Whether it is to be one or the other will depend largely upon the size of the group that wishes to present it, and the place where it is to be given.

Since the mask grew out of the Church, and since the Church provides a beautiful and dignified setting, naturally it becomes a most appropriate place for a Christmas mask. The Church has so much to offer that it is not surprising to find it again welcoming pageantry and the mask. The organist and choir provide the music, members with dramatic talent perform the pantomime, sewing groups make the costumes, while those who have a gift for crafts can make the masks and properties.

A Christmas mask, when given in a school, may require the coöperation of all departments. The English department may find the theme and place it in a period and give it dramatic form and train the reader and maskers in pantomime. In the art department, the masks will be made, the costumes and properties will be designed and decorated. The library furnishes books and plates. The sewing department makes the costumes. The wood-working department makes the properties. The music department finds appropriate music and trains the chorus. The printing department prints programs, posters, and tickets.

Here is an example of the plan and development of a Christmas mask given for children by the pupils of a junior high school. The first consideration was the size of the stage and its possibilities. The second consideration was the attention of the audience. It was thought that an entertainment that lasted an hour would not be too long. The problem then was to find or to make a story that would develop, reach its climax and conclusion within an hour. Naturally this story had to be dramatic, have a simple and clearly defined plot, and its characters few and vivid. The story chosen was laid in England in the XVth Century. The history, art, songs, and customs of that time seemed to lend themselves so readily to a mask. The theme chosen was unselfish love. The characters were the King, Queen, Sage, Lady-in-Waiting, Pages, Peasant Mother, and her son, St. George, the Dragon, the Doctor and Jack, the Giant Killer, and the Morris dancers. Beautiful old English carols were woven into the story, which was told by a reader, accompanied by a harp. The mask begins with the carol "Holy Night, Silent Night." This is sung by a concealed chorus of boys. The curtains open, the King is seated on his throne, his Counsellor and Page beside him. The reader begins a story of selfishness and greed that rule throughout the kingdom and with a dream of the unhappy King. The Sage opens his great book and counsels the King to send forth messengers to find if anyone in all the land has done an unselfish deed. This alone can save the kingdom. The scene closes with the departure of the pages and the singing of the carol: "We three Kings of the Orient are, bearing gifts, we have traveled afar."

The second scene is laid in a humble dwelling. Here an old peasant mother awaits the return of her son from his day's work. The reader tells the story of their poverty, and of the old mother's courage in facing the day when her son must leave her to go forth into the world. Distant carolers are heard singing:

Good King Wenceslaus looked out on the feast of Stephen.
While the snow lay round about deep and crisp and even.

As the carolers' voices die away, the son returns and tells a marvelous tale. He has saved the son of a nobleman from a wild boar and as a reward the nobleman offers to take him away to his great castle. The mother rejoices in his good fortune, though it means their separation. The son tells his mother that he has refused the reward in order to stay and take care of her.

They sit down to their humble meal, and bow their heads in thanksgiving. One of the King's messengers enters, tells of his futile quest and asks them if they have heard of anyone who has performed an unselfish deed. The mother tells of her son's devotion. The messenger rejoices and declares that in all his wanderings he has heard of nothing but selfishness. He bids them follow him to the court. As the curtains close, the chorus sings: "Joy to the World."

The third scene shows the King and Queen upon the throne, a Lady-in-Waiting and the Counsellor attending them. The unsuccessful messengers return, kneel before the throne, and sadly bow their heads. The triumphant messenger returns, bringing with him the old mother and her son. The reader tells the story of their devotion and there is general rejoicing. The King bestows blessings and favors and then sends for the mummers, who come in led by St. George and the Doctor with his great bottles of pills ("red to cure, and blue to kill") little Jack, the Giant Killer, the terrible Dragon, and the Morris dancers.

The mummers perform the old English play of St. George and the Dragon. The Morris men give the stick dance. At the close St. George and little Jack

beg pennies from the court, while the dancers go
begging through the audience and the chorus sings:

> Here we come a wassailing among the leaves so green.
> Here we come a wandering so fair to be seen.

The King steps forth and blesses all the people.
They kneel reverently as the Christmas chimes begin
to ring. The King and Queen now come down and
kneel with their people, while the chorus triumph-
antly sings: "Hark, the Herald Angels Sing, Glory to
the New-born King."

The Christmas mask illustrated in these pages was
written about the Crusade of St. Louis of France. It
sought to re-create, through music, pantomime, costumes, and dance, the spirit of the XIIIth Century.
It was inspired by the wealth of the material of this
period in the Cleveland Museum of Art. Here were
examples of Gothic sculpture which gave the note of
simplicity and reverence, and at the same time accurate information about pose, expression, costume, and
line. The stained-glass windows, enamels, and illuminated manuscripts gave suggestions for color and
color arrangement. Old Italian chests and the frames
of early Siennese paintings influenced the designs of
the necessary furniture. In the art library were found
photographs and plates of sculptures of the cathedrals of Chartres, Amiens, and Rheims. These were
studied for costumes, headdresses, ornaments, and
especially for the types of faces which were to be used
in the masks. Examples of early textiles were drawn
upon for designs of costumes and background.

The King collection of books on costume at the Cleveland Historical Society furnished references on costumes.

The rare John G. White collection of folklore and music in the Cleveland Public Library furnished songs and chronicles of the time. In this collection beautiful old French music of the XIth, XIIth, and XIIIth centuries was found. The songs were translated and adapted so that they could be sung by children. The action of the mask was made to take place on Christmas Eve, in the year 1255, in the hall of the castle of Count Mathew of Brittany. The mask began with a procession of forty children, in costume, singing this XIVth Century noel:

> Lead us, Lord, where He doth lie this night!
> There is a Child of Mary born!
> Salvation hath He brought to us,
> Whom we should worship night and morn.

> Lead us, Lord, a star now shineth bright!
> In Bethlehem it so befell
> That in a stable born He was
> Pray Him for grace to serve Him well.

> Show us, Lord, where angel wings are light!
> The shepherds heard that Angel-song
> That grace did bring from out the sky
> Where Man was born mankind among.

> Conditor, our Lord of Power and Might
> Now let each man upon Him call,
> Who sits enthroned in Heaven high,
> That to His bliss He bring us all.

Masks

Upper: *Mummer, Queen, Jester*
Middle: *Egyptian Priest, Persian Poet, Greek Maiden*
Lower: *Columbine and Pierrot*

These children made a beautiful picture as they grouped themselves before the tall trees at the right and left of the stage. With them sat the soloists and the orchestra. A reader dressed in the costume of the period told the story. A group of sixteen children, masked and costumed as the characters in the story, presented the pantomime.

This mask aimed to impress, through music and the harmony between spoken word and gesture, the deep significance of Christmas.

CHAPTER III

Making the Mask

ANYONE who has ever tried to make masks, knows their fascination. A pillowcase with two holes cut in it for eyes may have been your first mask. A paper bag may have been your second mask. What a wonderful chance this gave you to show your originality. You may remember how you labored to express some humorous or grotesque idea. There was the paper nose that you cut, fitted and glued to it, and the ears that you made for it, the mouth that you painted, and the headdress of feathers and quills. Above all, there was the joy of wearing it and of comparing your mask with the masks of your friends.

All masks reflect the ideas and feelings of those who make them. Great masks have individuality and character. How does one make a mask that has character? It is done in some such manner as this: First decide whether your mask is to represent an imaginary character or a historical character. If it is to represent an imaginary character you will have a great deal of freedom in working out your idea, for no one can say, exactly, what a goblin or demon or any fanciful creature looks like. But if your mask is to represent a historical character the problem is quite a different one. In that case you are guided by tradition and also by the structure and proportions of the human face.

Let us suppose that you wish to make a mask of a noble king. He probably would have a high forehead, a straight brow, a strong, firm chin, and a kindly mouth. Exaggerate the high forehead, the straight brow, the firm chin, and the kindliness of the mouth, and you will find that every one who sees your mask will be conscious of its nobility. Is your king young or old? If he is old, there will be hollows about his eyes, nose, and mouth, and his cheeks may be thin. If he is young, his flesh will be firm and there will be no drawn or sagging muscles. Exaggerate the roundness of youth and the thinness of old age, keeping the proportions and qualities which indicate nobility.

The brow indicates mood—surprise and curiosity are shown by arched eyebrows; sadness and grief are shown by drooping eyebrows; perplexity and anger are shown by the drawing together of the eyebrows.

The nose is very important and demands careful study. It should be consistent with the character. Can you imagine a noble, generous king with a short, upturned nose?

The mouth and chin are quite as important as the brow and nose. Beginners often have great difficulty in modeling them, because they forget to consider the profile. The lips and chin must be built out and shaped exactly like those of the human face.

When you have the character of this noble king well in mind, take a pencil and paper and make a sketch of him, front view and side view. Keep in mind the general proportions of his face. Having made your drawing you are ready to begin your work with clay. Measure your face from chin to the crown of the head, and the width of your face from ear to ear. Do this carefully, for a good mask should fit the face of the wearer. Onto a slate or a board crush some newspapers into a mound, about 4 by 6 inches, and 3 inches high. This paper, acting as a core, will

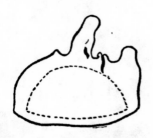

save your clay and insure its quick drying. Pack the clay over the paper as in the illustration, to a depth of about 6 inches. If the length of your face is $8\frac{1}{2}$ inches, make the mound of clay $8\frac{3}{4}$ inches, since the clay shrinks in drying. For the same reason, add an extra $\frac{1}{4}$ inch to the width. With your drawing before

Characters from Christmas Mask

you, begin modeling the clay. Remember that a face is not flat. Observe the plans of the forehead, the cheeks, and eye sockets. The expression which you imagine the noble king to have had should be modeled into the clay and the wrinkles cut into the forehead and about the mouth. You must study your mask from many angles in order to make it lifelike.

If you do not finish your modeling the first day, cover the clay with wet cloths to keep it from hardening. When you have completed your clay model it will require twenty-four to thirty-six hours for it to dry. From this model you are now ready to make either a papier-mâché mask or a buckram mask. If you wish to make a papier-mâché mask cover the model when thoroughly dry with a thin coat of vaseline. Now tear medium-weight wrapping paper, cream and brown for instance, into pieces three or four inches long, soak them in hot water, wring out separately, dip into flour paste, and rub gently between the fingers until they feel like wet chamois skin. Cover the entire surface with the cream-colored strips of paper. The pieces may overlap but there must be no wrinkles. When the entire surface is covered you may apply immediately a second layer. Let this be of the brown paper. Follow this with a third layer of cream and a fourth layer of brown. If your paper is thin, apply a fifth or even a sixth layer to give the necessary thickness and strength. The alternating of the cream and brown will help you to count your layers and insures uniform thickness. Strive to keep a smooth surface and a uniform thickness. Do not forget that in this process the last layer of paper becomes the outer surface of your mask. After twenty-four or thirty-six hours, the paper masks should be dry enough to remove from the clay. Plasticine may be used instead of clay but since it does not harden, this process necessitates making a plaster of Paris mold. The directions for making this are given on page 66.

When you have removed the paper mask from the clay or plaster mold, cut out the eye and nostril holes. If a mask is to be worn by a dancer, the lips should be modeled slightly opened to permit the cutting away of the paper between the lips.

If you decide to make a buckram mask you will require a piece of light-colored buckram about twice the size of the face. Soften the buckram with warm water, then place over the clay model which has been covered with a coat of soapsuds. Press the buckram carefully, so as to bring out all the modeling of the features, then allow to dry.

The next step is the construction of that part of the mask which will cover the head. Here you will need assistance. While you hold the mask to your face, your assistant will take a one-inch strip of heavy paper, long enough to go around the back of the head, and attach it to the outside edges of the mask, just above the ears. If this strip is attached too low, the mask cannot be removed from the head, if too high, the mask will not be held securely. You will soon discover that it is necessary to put the chin into the mask first, when you put it on. A mask should fit the face and head closely. If you follow the steps in the illustration, you will see how this basketlike framework is constructed and how any kind of headdress can be built up on it. When a headdress is completed, and the inside of the mask is finished with a lining of

papier-mâché, you are ready to paint the mask. Oil paints are the most practical. Tempora colors, however, may be used. The painting of the mask should emphasize the character.

Complexion is the first consideration. Faces usually are fair, sallow, or swarthy. There are certain masks, however, that are much more effective when they are painted symbolically. The mask of the priest of Osiris was painted a rich green to indicate the fertility of the Nile. The demon mask was painted a greenish-gray. Yellow, vermilion, and black were used to heighten the terrifying aspects. Observation and experiment will guide you in the painting of the eyes, lips, brow, and hair, and also in the subtle violet shadows about the eyes, cheeks, and chin. Beware of timid lines that imitate nature. They say very little when the mask is a few feet away from you. Big, sweeping rhythmic lines make for design and carrying power, and are to be seen in all great masks. The inside of the mask should also be painted, decorated if you like, and shellacked when the oil paint is thoroughly dry. This prevents the breath from softening the papier-mâché. The outside must not be shellacked.

The masks shown in the accompanying illustrations aimed to bring out the most important traits of the character chosen. North American Indian symbolism of design and color was carried out in the masks of the Corn Maidens. Each mask was made by a different person, with a very clear idea in mind of what she wished her mask to express. Notice how like and yet unlike these Corn Maiden masks are. A clown's face is supposed to show grotesque humor. By exaggerating nose, ears, and mouth, both in shape and color, the grotesque effects of the clown group were produced. Cheerfulness and contented old age are characterized by two Oriental masks shown at the bottom of the page. The demon mask grew out of a careful study of Chinese and Japanese demon masks.

The remoteness and dignity of ancient Egypt are reflected in the mask of the Priest of Osiris. The poetical sensitiveness of the mask of an Oriental poet was inspired by the faces in early Persian miniatures. There is much of wistfulness and subtle character delineation in the mask of the jester. This mask was worn with a parti-colored costume, cap and bells.

The possibilities of character masks are suggested by the photographs of the "Christmas Masque" given by the children's singing classes of the Cleveland Museum of Art, and by the ninth grade special art class of Fairmount Junior High School, assisted by the Music School Settlement at the Cleveland Museum of Art, Christmas, 1925.

CHAPTER IV

The Costume and Setting for the Mask

COSTUME is a means of introducing characters, of telling time and place, and of creating dramatic mood. A costume should be different from ordinary clothes, and should have a characteristic quality that will help an actor to interpret his part. Imagine Charlie Chaplin in any other outfit than his own. Do you think this costume of his came by chance? Much thought and experiment went into its creation. Have you ever noticed how this artist wears his shabby, droll, almost pathetic costume, and how he uses it to play upon your feelings? His work is an illustrious example of a great artist's use of costume.

There are two kinds of costumes, those which grow out of pure imagination and those which reproduce

168

the costumes worn in different periods in different countries. The latter are spoken of as period costumes. Under imaginative costumes come those of Maeterlinck's *Blue Bird* which represent fire, water, milk, sugar, bread, and those of the old morality plays, such as virtue, vice, modesty, poverty, envy, and greed.

Imaginative Costumes. Three things are essential to the imaginative costume: appropriate line, appropriate color, and appropriate material. The kind of costume that would represent wind would require drapery, the lines of which would suggest the movement of wind when the body was in motion. Water, however, would require straight, downward falling lines. The color of an imaginative costume is important. Who can imagine a fairy in black or a gnome in white, a character representing spring in russet brown or one representing autumn in yellow-green? Materials likewise have their appropriate uses. Fairies are not weighted down with velvet, neither are gnomes given costumes of gauze.

Period Costumes. When we come to period costumes, accurate information is necessary. The quest leads us to libraries, with their illustrated books, photographs, and plates; to historical and art museums with whatever they may have of original material.

North American Indian Costumes. One costume that is familiar to every American boy and girl is that of the North American Indian. We occasionally see Indians at the circus, as traveling medicine men, or on their reservations. Many museums are making collections of their costumes and their arts. Government publications, such as the beautifully illustrated

Indian Costumes

Warrior   *Maiden*   *Chief*

ethnological reports, with information about almost every tribe, are in most libraries. Many libraries have the wonderful Curtis photographs. The *National Geographic* and other magazines have illustrations that could also be used.

Considering the dramatic part that the Indian has played in American life, what subject could be more appropriate for a mask? Indian life and legend offer an equally vivid and colorful opportunity for the mask. The wealth of material is inspiring. Every community in our country can find somewhere in its history stirring events related to Indian life. What could be more interesting than to weave these incidents of pioneer life into masks? These could be presented by school clubs and boy and girl scout troops, in parks and playgrounds.

Israelite Costumes

Priest   *Maiden*   *Tribesman*

Bible Costumes. A mask with characters taken from the Bible could be very beautifully costumed. One could use pictures of the artist, Tissot, who spent many years of his life in Palestine, sketching costumes that he felt were similar to those of Bible times. His illustrations show how widely the rich Eastern costumes differ from our own. The materials used were fine, transparent linen and silk and cloth made from wool and camels' and goats' hair. The various classes of people were distinguished by difference in the richness, costliness, and simplicity of their dress. Ornament is very characteristic of all these Oriental costumes. The sculptured figures on one of the tombs near Thebes show the Israelites brought before their Egyptian conquerors wearing fringed garments. Moses commanded that fringe be worn by his people. This was probably a survival of a still more ancient usage in the family of Jacob. Assyrian reliefs show Israelite captives being stripped of their ornaments, sandals, anklets, embroidered robes and tunics, girdles and armlets, thin veils, caps of network, ear pendants, bracelets, rings, and jewels of the nose.

Egyptian Costumes. The costumes of the ancient Egyptians may easily come into a mask of Bible times. Materials used were fine linen, cotton, and wool. The common people wore merely a piece of linen tied around the loins. Occasionally the skin of a tiger or leopard was thrown over the shoulders. Both men and women wore broad collars around the neck and over the breast. The men wore armlets, bracelets, and finger rings, while the women added to these or-

Egyptian Costumes

God Osiris   Princess   King

naments, diadems, girdles, and bands of ornament around the breast and hips. The headdress was important, for it indicated the rank of the wearer. The illustration shows the characteristic features of their costumes.

Cretan Costumes. If you have ever felt that the ancient costume lacked what we call "style," behold this snappy, chic little Cretan goddess! With her short-sleeved, closely fitting jacket, full flounced skirt and wasp waist, headgear, loops, and sashes. She

173

Cretan Goddess

might have been the very latest word from Paris a generation ago.

Greek Costumes. When we speak of Greek costumes, we usually think of those upon Greek statues, such as the Athena and Artemis. Since these are in marble or in plaster of Paris, it is quite natural that we should think of the Greek costume as being white. It is interesting to learn, however, that Greek costumes showed a great variety of colors.

The favorite colors were deep purple, red, and

174

yellow. There was a very dark blue and a green described as the color of unripe grapes or frog colored. The materials used were linen, wool, sometimes cot-

Greek Costumes: Man and Woman

ton, and silk. The costumes worn by the common people were of coarsely woven wool. The finest weaving was worn by the people of wealth. Design was important in the Greek costume. Sometimes it was an all-over symmetrical pattern or a floral or an animal pattern. Even the human figure was used as a motif. A fragment having a naturalistic design of

175

ducks embroidered in gold and green on a dark brown background has been found. These designs were sometimes woven into the material, sometimes embroidered, and very frequently painted upon the materials. Border designs beaten out in thin gold were not infrequently stitched onto the dress.

The chief and indispensable garment of a Greek woman was her peplos, which was a piece of material sewed together, open at top and bottom, and reaching from the neck to the feet. The width was equal to the extended arms. It was fastened over the shoulders with a kind of pin or fibula and about the waist with a girdle. Under this she wore a short undergarment. A similar but much shorter and simpler chiton was sometimes worn by the Greek men. The outer garment for both men and women was a kind of cloak or mantle made from an oblong of wool, 7 or 8 feet long by 5 or 6 feet wide. There were many ways of wearing this garment which was called the "himation." Here is a description of the toilet of the Goddess Hera: "Then she clad her in her fragrant robe, that Athena wrought delicately for her, and therein set many things beautifully made, and fastened it over her breast with clasps of gold. And she girdled it with a girdle arrayed with a hundred tassels, and she set earrings in her pierced ears—earrings of three drops and glistening—and therefrom shone grace abundantly. And with a veil over all, the peerless goddess veiled herself—a fair, new veil, bright as the sun, and beneath her shining feet she bound goodly sandals." (Lang, Leaf, & Myers.)

Roman Costumes. Roman dress was patterned after the Greek. It was unbelievably ample. The toga was a huge elliptical piece of cloth in length three times

Roman Costumes

Soldier   Lady   Noble

the height of the person who wore it and in width twice his height. Imagine the skill required to arrange this garment. The toga was of thin white woolen stuff. When bordered with purple, it denoted a person holding public office. A purple toga was always a mark of high office. It was sometimes embroidered in gold. Under the toga was worn a short garment called

177

Dominicans or Black Friars wore similar habit to that worn by the Augustine monks.

Franciscans or Gray Friars wore long, loose gray

Ecclesiastical Costumes

Bishop   *Nun*   *Monk*

cassocks girded with a cord, a hood or cowl, and a cloak of the same.

Carmelite or White Friars wore habits of white throughout, but from about 1240 to 1290 their cloaks were parti-colored, white and red.

Crossed Friars wore blue habits with a plain red cross.

In the early church there were various orders of nuns. They lived in convents, apart from the world, and took the vows of poverty, chastity, and obedience. Their costumes were of extreme simplicity and dignity, in keeping with their religious ideas. Each order had a distinctive costume of gray, blue, brown, white, or black. The materials were wool and linen. Note the full mantle, sleeves, and head-covering.

Crusaders' Costumes. Every boy and girl who loves adventures has no doubt been thrilled by stories of the Crusaders. The story of Richard the Lion-hearted may come to your mind. This illustration shows you the kind of costumes that he and other Crusaders wore. Beginning in the year 1096, and during the two hundred years which followed, there were nine crusades. People from every country in Europe and from every class set forth for the conquest of Jerusalem and the recovery of the Holy Sepulcher. When these great companies of people set forth each wore the costume of his own country and class, but upon each surcoat was worn the cross. According to the order of Pope Urban II which read: "You are a soldier of the Cross, wear, then, on your shoulder the blood-red sign of Him who died for the salvation of your souls." What a sight it must have been! Godfrey of Bouillon set forth from his province of Lorraine with 10,000 horsemen and 80,000 infantry, all bearing this blood-red cross upon their surcoats. Raymond of Tou-

Crusader's Costume

louse led forth, it is said, with 160,000 horse and foot.

Out of the successes and failures of these great pilgrimages came the experience and inspiration that created the literature, architecture, and arts of the Middle Ages, and gave the Christian world many of its saints and martyrs.

XIIIth Century Costumes. One of the greatest expressions of this intensely religious age was the cathedrals. From the infinite number of statues that are carved upon their façades and especially their portals and those statues that are within the cathedrals, from the figures in their stained-glass windows, the brass effigies in their pavements, and their frescoes and paintings, came the most authentic and complete

XIIth Century Costumes: Lady and Noble'

information about the costumes of this period. Illuminated manuscripts and tapestries, such as the Bayeaux tapestry, are also valuable sources. Photographs and reproductions of all this material are available. If one is seriously interested in costume he can collect reproductions from a surprising number of sources, such as newspapers, especially the Sunday supplement, magazines, and postcards, and make them into a costume scrapbook.

The history of England from the time of William the Conqueror to that of King John and Magna Carta furnishes a wealth of material for the mask. Stories of William the Conqueror, Robin Hood and his Merry Men, the Canterbury Pilgrims and Ivanhoe, will come to your mind. English costumes show little change from the IXth to the XIVth Century. The men wore a sleeved tunic, rather short, partly open at the sides, confined by a girdle. Over this tunic, usually very plain, was worn a mantle. It was a universal custom to cross-bandage the legs from the knee down. Pointed caps and shoes or low boots were worn. Women wore long tunics or gowns with close-fitting sleeves, made loose and girt in about the waist. A short tunic with very wide sleeves at the wrist was worn over this. This garment was often richly embroidered. For the out of doors there was an extra mantle with hood. Beautiful ornaments of gold and bronze were worn by both men and women. Coverchiefs were worn over the head, encircling the face and covering the throat and shoulders. The coverchief later became the wimple. Women wore their hair flowing or in two braids brought forward over the shoulders. The men wore flowing hair and the two-pointed beard. The garments of royal persons were made of very rich materials.

An illuminated portrait of Eleanor of Acquitaine represents her "with a wimple with a circlet of gems; her under tunic fitting closely and having tight sleeves is gathered into a rich collar about her throat; over this dress is a long tunic, loose and flowing, bordered

XIIIth Century Costumes: Lady and Noble

with ermine, its full and open sleeves being lined with fur; and over all, there is the ever-present mantle so adjusted that at the pleasure of the wearer it might be drawn over the head."

Richard the Lion-hearted wore over a white under tunic a longer tunic and an almost equally long crimson dalmatic slit up at the sides. The latter garment had very full sleeves. The mantle of royal blue and gold was fastened in the center over the chest by a large morse. He wore gloves jeweled at the back of

184

the hand, and enriched boots with spurs attached with buckled straps.

Here is a description of a XIIIth Century costume of King John. At a certain Christmas festival he appeared in a white damask tunic with jeweled girdle and gloves, his mantle being of red satin embroidered with sapphires and pearls.

XVth Century Costumes. Romances and ballads founded upon tales of chivalry are colorful material

XVth Century Costumes: Lady and Noble

for the mask. These are most frequently laid in the XIVth and XVth centuries. This was the time when heraldry was at its height and there was great interest in armorial devices. These appeared on the rich cos-

XVIth Century Costumes: Lady and Noble

tumes of the time, which were made from silk, satin, velvet, and cloth of gold. Women wore very long and full skirts, tight waists and sleeves. Rows of buttons appear on waists and sleeves. There is a loose girdle about the hips. The horned, steeple, and butterfly headdresses were most extravagant. Shoes had long, pointed toes. Long mantles were popular. The costumes of the men of the same century consisted of a tight-fitting tunic with tight sleeves, rows of buttons, loose girdle, long hose, shoes with pointed toes. Mantles were of the richest materials and these were splendidly adorned.

XVIth Century Costumes. Masks founded on the life of Columbus and the discovery of America will require costumes following those of the XVIth Century. The costume for men show trunk hose, a jerkin or jacket closed at the throat, sleeves cut and slashed, and a very short coat that was called a doublet. In addition to this there was a very full cloak or cape that hung from the shoulder; a little flat cap was worn with this costume. Short hair came into style early in this century. Women wore full skirts, sometimes extended by a kind of wheellike frame of whalebone that was known as a "farthingale," tight waists, puffed and slashed sleeves, and wide muffs. The world was ransacked to find stuffs to satisfy the extravagance of the XVIth Century.

The colonial history of the United States is rich in material for pageants and masks. What could be more vivid and interesting than the story of the Pilgrims, Dutch founders of New York, or of the Cavaliers of Virginia? The costumes of these periods are well known to you.

The Cavalier of the XVIIth Century continued the extravagance of the XVIth Century. His hat was wide brimmed and befeathered. There was lace at his neck, wrist, and boot top. His doublet let his fine cambric shirt be seen at the waist.

The women were equally elegant. Loose sleeves

XVIIth Century Costumes: Cavalier and Lady

were turned up at the elbows with bows of ribbon. A tight-fitting bodice came down over a full skirt divided in front to show an elaborate underskirt. A wide collar covered the shoulders. This was a time of patches, hair powder, face paints, great feather fans, and muffs of fur, and the wearing of small black masks, presumably as a protection from the sun.

The costume of the XVIIth Century most familiar to us is that of the Pilgrim. It reflects the protest against the worldliness and extravagance of the time. The hat was wide-brimmed and high-crowned, with

XVIIth Century Pilgrim Costumes

a wide ribbon band. Plain, wide collars of linen fell over the shoulders of their simply cut garments, which were of home-spun linen or wool. Not all Pilgrims wore somber gray, brown, or black. Many chose deep red, blue, or plum color.

The characteristic features of the XVIIIth Century costume of the French court during the reign of Louis XV and Louis XVI are shown in the high ornate head, dress of the women, the small waist, the wide flounced skirt, the exquisite silk brocades, jeweled and painted fans. The men of this period wore as elegant costumes

XVIIIth Century Court Costumes

as the women and gave much thought to their wigs, laces, and snuffboxes.

The Colonial costume followed the XVIIth Century costume in America. It was directly influenced by the fashions set by Louis XV and Louis XVI. The costumes of the men of fashion of the colonies were made from satins, laces, and embroideries imported from France. Their periwigs and their enameled and jeweled snuffboxes were also French. The ladies of this period were equally exquisite. They wore full-flounced skirts over huge whaleboned petti-

XVIIIth Century Colonial Costumes

coats and tight bodices. Sloping shoulders, powdered wigs, painted faces, and patches were the fashion.

When you have decided upon the costume you wish to make, then comes the very practical problem of materials. These need not be expensive since satines, unbleached muslin, cambric, tarlatan, cheesecloth, and oilcloth can be made to give beautiful effects. The advantages of satine are that it has body and texture and comes in a great range of colors. It has the sheen of satin, and is fairly inexpensive. It can be block printed or stenciled with gold, silver, or colors, and made to resemble the richest fabrics. Cambric is less expensive, but has less body and texture. It, too, can be made very effective by block printing or stenciling. Designs taken from fine old textiles in museums or from books or plates can be sketched or traced and then adapted for stencil or block.

Cloth of gold or silver can be made by painting muslin, gauze, or net with gold or silver radiator paint. This can be stenciled by brushing the stencil pattern with rabbit's foot glue, then removing the stencil and sprinkling the design with gold or silver powder. There are no materials more satisfactory than unbleached muslin or cheesecloth when they have been dyed. These are very inexpensive. The dyeing is not difficult and gives beautiful results for the small amount of time and effort spent. The better standard dyes are very satisfactory, and can be used either hot or cold. By combining the dyes in the same way that you would mix pigments (see page 94) you can produce any true tint or shade that you wish.

Rich effects are often produced by a second and third dipping. Very often colored cheesecloth gains by being redipped. As an illustration, a piece of blue cheesecloth dipped in a green dye bath becomes a lovely blue-green. Experiment with small pieces of your material before you dip the larger pieces.

The accessories of costumes, such as chains, brooches, girdles, and scabbards are often necessary.

Beads of glass, wood, clay, macaroni, and various seeds can be painted, enameled, or gilded, and set into papier-mâché for crowns, brooches, bracelets, and earrings. Buttons and glass ornaments can be used in the same way.

The design of a costume must be considered even more than its materials. A designer is an artist who uses fabric, color, and line to create an impression and to express an idea. He should study the play, and understand its dramatic ideas and moods. If he does this, his costumes will be as expressive, if properly worn, as the words of the actors.

Historic costumes reflect in a remarkable way the life, tastes, and feelings of an earlier time. But historic costumes also require an artist to reproduce them. The designer of an historic costume should know a great deal about the people who first wore this particular kind of costume and why they wore it. He will then choose suitable materials and colors, and will try to reproduce characteristic lines and silhouettes.

Last but not least comes the wearing of a costume. This requires two very important things: intelligence and imagination. The wearer, as well as the designer, should know the life, customs, and manners of the period which the costume represents. If he does not know them how can he move and gesture and assume the characteristic attitudes which the period demands and bring the costume into harmonious relation with the setting?

A mask requires but few properties. A throne, a

chair, or a stool may be sufficient, if well designed and of the proper period. A rich, colorful hanging or rug against a neutral background will draw your stage picture together and add dignity to a scene.

The throne and stool shown in the photograph on page 178 were made from beaver board, after designs of Gothic furniture. The design was first drawn on the beaver board; to the design were then glued pieces of rope clothesline, while small rolls of papier-mâché were glued on for the lowest relief. The entire surface was then covered with pieces of unbleached muslin which had been soaked in whiting, glue, and warm water. When this was dry a coat of dark earth-brown oil paint was applied. Lastly a small amount of gold was rubbed over the design. The result resembled rich carved wood.

Much can be done with papier-mâché in the making of minor properties, such as croziers, maces, harps, lutes, jewel boxes, helmets, shields, sword handles, and scabbards. Properties should add to the beauty of a scene, never dominate it. They will be much more convincing when they suggest rather than minutely imitate the actual object. A background may be no more than a box hedge and still be most charming.

Everyone is familiar with the beauty of woodland settings. Masks of spring, summer, and the harvest time of Shakespearean plays almost demand some such setting.

Masks of winter bring us indoors. Possibly the best indoor background is the simple gray curtain of velvet, velveteen, monks' cloth, outing flannel, or cambric. Against it costumes are seen to advantage and lights of all colors may be thrown against it successfully.

Since a mask is a highly conventionalized form of drama, it is possible to use a background painted with appropriate decorative or symbolic designs. An illustration of this is the symbolic pine tree painted on the wall of the temple courtyard for the Japanese *No* dramas. Screens of various kinds are full of possibilities. In the church or Sunday school, classroom, auditorium, library, or settlement, in the yard, playground, or park, ingenuity, imagination, and taste will always create a fitting background.

CHAPTER V

The Mask with Pantomime, Music, and Dance

THE wearing of masks made it difficult for the Greek actors to speak their lines. Naturally they came to rely upon gestures quite as much as upon words to carry their meaning to the audience. This interpretation by gesture led to the development of the art of pantomime.

The great pantomimists had wit and humor. They knew how to take a story and improve it in the telling. Their hands expressed more than their words, and their gestures were a language that all understood. Masks made it possible for each actor to assume different rôles, and his mimicking was in keeping with the character of the mask he wore.

It was no unusual thing in the Greek towns and cities to see a jolly company of these mimes and musicians in grotesque costumes, their faces masked or smeared with soot, riding in chariots through the streets so that they might advertise their plays.

These plays were little dramas and comedies in which pantomime and music played an important part.

Pantomime was popular with the Romans and for this reason despised by the early Christians. It survived, nevertheless, through a few obscure actors and mountebanks. Gradually these mimics and their fellows banded themselves together. They appeared at festivals whenever they were summoned, only to disappear afterward into the deep obscurity of a stroller's life.

The mimics, or jongleurs (as they were called in France in the early Middle Ages), kept alive the tradition of dramatic entertainment. Among the famous mimics was Taillefer, who rode into the battle of Hastings tossing his sword into the air and catching it again, while he sang songs of Roland and Charlemagne. In France and in England the pantomimist was welcome in castle, in convent, and on village green.

From the Vth Century on, the Church gave much thought to forms of dramatic public worship, and sought thereby to interest and instruct the people. Living pictures, accompanied by songs, were used to illustrate the gospel narrative. On great festival days, such as Christmas, Good Friday, and Easter, the priests performed in pantomime the incidents appropriate to the occasion. Out of these very simple rites grew the mysteries, miracles, and the elaborate morality plays in which pantomime played a very important part.

In addition to such sacred plays, there were no end

of secular plays. These were given all over Europe by townsfolk and peasants, in the streets, at the fairs, and in the great halls of the castles. Among the most popular of the English folk plays were the St. George plays. These were acted at Christimas time by bands of masked townsmen and peasants who called themselves mummers. Several versions of these old St. George plays, which can still be adapted and used in a Christmas mask, have come down to us. Among the characters are St. George, the Doctor, Little Jack, Father Christmas, the old dragon, and the Morris men.

In Italy during the XVIth and XVIIth centuries there was a popular form of character comedy that was known as the *Commedia dell' arte*. This was performed by bands of professional actors who strolled about the country giving their improvised plays to any chance audience. As time went on and their popularity grew, the more clever of these bands established themselves in theaters in the towns and cities, where they gave a great variety of performances. The principal characters of their plays were Harlequin, Scaramouch, Columbine, Pantalone, and Punchinello. These characters all wore masks and were adepts in the art of pantomime. These Italian musicians and actors of the *Commedia dell' arte* traveled to Spain, France, and finally to England, where their boisterous humor was warmly welcomed by high and low. Here is an account of one part of the festivities that were given in Kenilworth, in the year 1576:

"Noow within allso . . . waz thear showed before her Highness by an Italian, such feats of agilitie, in goinges, turninges, tumblinges, castinges, hops, jumps, leaps, skips, springs, gambauds, soomersaults, caprittiez and flights; forward, backward, sydewize, a downward, upward, and with sundry windings, gyrings and circumflexions; allso lightly and with such easiness, as by me in feaw words it is not expressible by pen or speech ... I bleast me by my faith to behold him, and began to doout whither a waz a man or a spirite. . . . Az for thiz fellow I cannot tell what to make of him, save that I may geese his back be metalld like a lamprey, that haz no bones but a line like a lute-string."[2]

Pantomime was popular in England during the Reformation and morality plays were given in dumb show.

French actors were greatly influenced by these clever traveling Italian artists. They set up similar plays at their great fairs and finally established a theater in Paris, in which music and pantomime were developed to the highest perfection.

Until recent years nearly all that we have known of the great tradition of pantomime came to us through the circus clowns. Among these were a few artists such as Grimaldi, who never allowed their art to become low and trivial.

Now, all this is quite changed, since the coming of the movie. The moving picture depends entirely upon pantomime for interpreting character and expressing emotion. The greatest of the movie actors are great pantomimists. When we study the movements and gestures and the facial expressions of such actors as

Emil Jannings and Charlie Chaplin, we begin to understand what pantomime really is. Chaliapin is another great actor who understands the art of pantomime and uses it in opera.

Let us see how pantomime, music, and dance were used in the Christmas mask described at the end of chapter II "Occasions for Wearing the Mask." Masks for this play had been made for the following characters: a dignified king, a mournful queen, a gentle lady-in-waiting, an austere learned bishop, a faithful son, a clever jester, a rollicking band of mummers. Each pupil had made his own mask after very thorough study of the character that he had chosen. Knowing his character well enabled each student to interpret that character when he put on his mask, and for the time of the play, each student sought to become that character, king, queen, bishop, or mummer. The problem for each actor was that of bringing his movements and gestures into harmony with his mask. The king's movements should be no less dignified and stately than his mask suggested. The unhappy queen must express the sadness of her mask by her drooping head and shoulders and by her impassive hands. Her mask was so modeled that when lifted, it suggested a smile. This expression was required when she lifted her head in joy at her son's return.

The lady-in-waiting used pantomime to interpret her gentleness and modesty and the music which accompanied her XIIIth Century song. This song, sung off stage by one of the chorus, was singularly appropriate to the pensive quality of her mask.

LADY-IN-WAITING'S SONG

Though the winter be a-cold
Safe the lamb lies in the fold
   Roses red are sleeping
'Neath the brown earth deep and warm.
Spring at last with winter's storm
   Steals now so gently creeping.

Soon the rose will bloom and blow,
Soon the birds sing loud and low.
   Love hath breathed not coldly.
Deep in dungeon underground,
Love the knight hath fastly bound.
   To these he strideth boldly.

Thou bereft and all alone
By our Lady Mary's Son,
   Weep ye not so sadly!
Of his true love, found again
Never knight was half so fain.
   Look! now He cometh gladly.

The jester used pantomime in his dance. His inspiration for his poses came from the illustrations in old manuscripts and reproductions of old manuscripts. He sketches these, and then, assisted by a teacher who understood folk dancing, he worked out every step and pose to the music of this, his song:

JESTER'S SONG

Here am I, the Count's good fool.
   (Ch.) Aye, aye, ah,
Laughter is my only rule.
   (Ch.) Aye, aye, ah.
Tears alone do wake my rage.
   (Ch.) Aye, aye, ah.
With a smile I gain my wage.
   For jollity am I a page.

Chorus:

O, for joy! O, for joy!
Ah, to thee we dance
  To thee we dance,
  To thee we dance.
With many a wink and glance
  At Merriment's fool.

List my bauble's tinkling noise,
  (Ch.) Aye, aye, ah.
Kingly crowns my golden toys.
  (Ch.) Aye, aye, ah.
Here, with gallant, blythesome pose,
  (Ch.) Aye, aye, ah.
Leap I high upon my toes
To offer my lady a rose.

Chorus:

What can the mask, the age-old form of entertainment, give us to-day? It is so far from mere representation that it allows us to escape from realism and to enter freely into the world of fine and subtle character interpretation. It is a form of entertainment that lends itself to humor, to dignity, and to beauty, and enlists the finest creative effort.

SHADOWS

CHAPTER I

The Mystery of the Shadow

THE life of primitive man was full of peril. Out of the struggle to survive the dangers which threatened him on every side came fear and superstition. He developed a great regard for shadows which he could not understand. They were mysterious, they moved and changed, appeared and disappeared. They eluded him and yet pursued him. The shadow became for him a living thing. Gradually he came to look upon his own shadow as his very soul. He felt that he must shield and protect it. Consequently he would permit no one to step upon it, or even to touch it.

Stories of regard for the shadow come from many lands. The natives of Nias, an island in the Dutch East Indies, greatly feared the rainbow, because to them it was a powerful net set by a great spirit to catch their shadows, and to destroy them.

Savages of Wetar, a neighboring island, believe that a man can be made ill unto death if his shadow is stabbed, while the Ottawa Indians believed that a man will die if certain figures are drawn upon his shadow, and the Bushmen of Australia never allow their shadows to fall upon dead game. They are confident that bad luck will follow them if they do so. When a Malay builds a house, he takes the greatest care to prevent his shadow from falling into the hole that is being dug for the center post. If, by chance, his shadow should fall into the hole, he feels certain that sickness and trouble will follow him.

Here is a curious tale that comes from India. A priest named Saukara disagreed with the grand lama. In order to show his supernatural powers he soared far up into the sky, his long shadow falling on the ground. When the lama saw this shadow moving along on the ground, he drew out his sword and struck it. Saukara fell to the earth.

In Africa, the natives believe that even trees must guard their shadows. This is especially true of the trees that have medicinal leaves. A Kaffir doctor runs up very quickly to one of these medicinal trees and tries to avoid stepping on its shadow lest the shadow inform the tree of his coming and give it time to withdraw the healing properties of its leaves into the trunk.

One of the strangest customs that has existed since the time of the Greeks is still practised in southeastern

Europe. It is that of measuring a strong man's shadow and then of building the measuring line into the foundations of a building. The people believe that the strength of the man goes into the structure. In Roumania one frequently hears when passing a building under construction this warning cry: "Beware lest they take thy shadow." There are certain people who go about stealthily measuring the shadows of strong men. They sell these shadow measuring lines to the architects.

Gradually the superstitious fear of shadows passed. In the place of this fear came an interest in using shadows for entertainment. This may have been suggested by the shadows that fell on the walls of the sacred tent while the priests within were performing the holy rites.

Shadow plays originated in the Orient and are known in every Eastern country. Here is a tale of their Chinese origin. An emperor grew angry with his two court fools, and ordered their heads cut off. When his anger cooled, he began to feel that life was dull. He then ordered his grand vizier to bring his fools back to life. At this command, the vizier was almost at his wit's end for he knew that he would lose his own head if he could not fulfil the royal command. One day he met a fisherman with two great fishes. It suddenly occurred to him that he might take the skins of these fishes, dry them, and cut out from them two figures that would look like the two jesters. He succeeded in doing this, and after much thought and labor, he was able once more to show the Emperor his fools, this time as shadows against a lighted curtain, acting for his entertainment. These shadows seemed to please the Emperor even more than the living jesters.

In all Eastern countries the people usually prefer flat shadow figures to round marionettes. Such shadow figures are made from the carefully prepared skin of a goat or buffalo. After it has been stretched and dried, a clever artist takes the translucent skin and cuts out from it figures which represent the gods and heroes of the people. The illustration shows a characteristic Javanese shadow figure. The elaborate pattern is made by means of many small holes of different shapes and sizes. This figure is further enriched with transparent colors and gold. The arms are jointed at the shoulder and the elbow. Slender rods of wood, bone, or ivory are then fastened to the body and arms. The puppeteer manipulates the figure by means of these rods which extend below the figure. The shapes of the figures are most interesting, as you can see, with their strange headdresses, long noses, thin arms and legs. Their gestures are so grotesque and fascinating that they are like the strange people one meets only in dreams.

The theaters in which these shadow figures are shown are often no more than an angle of two walls before which is hung an opaque curtain in which there is a small opening with a bit of very fine linen stretched over it. This is lighted from behind. Here the showman sits with his figures all about him. And a very clever fellow he must be! Think of all the things he must do. First, he must know by heart all the stories that the people may wish to see acted, then he must know how to make the proper speech for each of his puppets, as well as how to make it act its part with the proper feeling and gestures. Further, he must be able to direct the orchestra of several men playing tomtoms, to manage his lights, and to shuffle his feet when that is necessary.

Can you guess how many puppets belong to his set? Count the characters in your favorite plays. If you take a long play like Shakespeare's *Midsummer Night's Dream*, and include a great band of fairies, there will scarcely be more than fifty characters. This showman has from sixty to one hundred and twenty shadows in his set. He must know just where every one is placed so that he can put his hand upon it the moment it is needed. He must also please people of many different tastes, therefore he must be able to give serious plays; plays about the gods, about giants and dragons, elves and fairies. Besides all of this he must know a great many hero plays, for it is through his art that the great heroes are kept alive.

Omar Khayyam, the Persian poet, compared life itself to a shadow show.

> For in and out, above, about, below,
> Life's nothing but a Magic Shadow-show.
> Play'd in a Box whose Candle is the Sun,
> Round which we Phantom Figures come and go.

The shadow figures of Oriental countries differ widely. For example, those of China are as beautiful in pattern and in color as those of the Javanese but are much less grotesque. The Turkish shadow figures are less beautiful than the Chinese and Javanese figures. They are very cleverly articulated, however, and so skilfully manipulated that they furnish the most common and popular form of dramatic entertainment. Black Eye or *Karagheuz* is the rogue hero, and is known throughout Turkey and the whole of northern Africa. The Karagheuz shows are the usual attraction of Greek and Turkish coffee houses.

Among the many things that came to Europe through trading with the Orient were Chinese shadow figures. They probably reached England early in the XVIth Century.

We know that the clever showman, Powell, used motions or shadows in his *Old Creation of the World with the Addition of Noah's Flood*, in 1641. More than a century later Chinese shadow plays came under royal favor in France. There they have been changed and adapted in many ways. The modern French shadow plays are pretentious, with many scenes and numerous characters. All the countries of Europe have made some use of the cut-out shadow figures.

Recently cut-out shadow figures have found a rival. This has come about through the growing appreciation of the dramatic possibilities of the human shadow figure. Modern lighting has done much toward this end, because it has made possible a clearly defined silhouette on the shadow screen.

The art of the human shadow is not limited. It

Upper: Scene from cut out shadow play, "The Traveling Musicians of Bremen."

Lower: Behind the scenes in a cut out shadow play, given by eighth grade pupils of Fairmount Junior High School, Cleveland, Ohio.

uses acting, dancing, music, the voice, and color. With a sense of design and arrangement, a beautiful picture is created before the audience every moment. The human shadow play is a new challenge to imagination, taste, and ingenuity.

CHAPTER II

Making a Shadow Play

IT IS not at all difficult to make a shadow play if one knows what the requirements are. The first requirement of either a cut-out shadow play or a human play is that its story shall have action. In this it is like a movie. You will recall how keenly you enjoy the action in such movies as *Robin Hood* and the *Black Pirate*. The second requirement is a dramatic plan or problem. This is necessary in order to hold the attention of the audience. For example, the dramatic plan or problem in the *Black Pirate* is the struggle of the hero to free himself from the pirates. Your attention is held by this struggle. The third requirement is the selection of the most important and interesting characters in the play. Since the success of a shadow play depends upon interesting silhouettes, each character must have individuality. No two silhouettes should be alike, either in appearance or size. As an illustration of this, notice that the shadow figures at the top of page 215 are of different appearance and height. Lastly, the settings of a shadow play should be very simple and suggestive and help to tell the story.

Nursery rhymes and fables, folk and fairy tales are delightful material for cut-out shadow plays. They are vivid, humorous, and fanciful. They are full of direct conversation which can be carried on by the puppeteers behind the screen or by a reader in front of the screen. In the following list you may find a story to turn into a cut-out shadow play. Nursery rhymes such as: *Little Bo Peep, Old King Cole, The Knave of Hearts, A Frog Who Would A-Wooing Go,* and *The House That Jack Built.* Fables such as those of Æsop, La Fontaine, and Bidpai. Folk and fairy tales, such as: *Cinderella, Beauty and the Beast, Jack and the Beanstalk, The Three Little Pigs, The Elves and the Shoemaker, Seven at a Blow, Snow White and the Dwarfs, The Three Bears, Red Riding Hood, Aladdin and His Wonderful Lamp, Sleeping Beauty, The Mermaid, Just-So Stories, Three Billy Goats Gruff, The Traveling Musicians of Bremen,* and *The Pied Piper of Hamelin Town.* Bible stories can be turned into beautiful shadow plays. For example, David and Goliath, Daniel in the Lion's Den, Jonah and the Whale, and Joseph and His Brethren.

Tales of heroism and adventure, ballads and poems, stories of Christmas and Easter, Bible stories and stories of the lives of the saints are appropriate for human shadow plays because they have great human interest and give opportunity for dramatic interpretation. The following list may be a guide to you in choosing your play: William Tell, Robin Hood, King Arthur, Roland and Oliver, Hiawatha, The Cid, Joseph and His Brethren, The Story of Moses, David and Jonathan, David Before Saul, The Good Samaritan, The Story of Ruth, The Story of Queen Esther, The Story of St. Francis of Assisi, The Nativity, The Christ-child Legend, Where Love Is There God Is. Also, and Christmas carols such as: Good King Wenceslaus, We Three Kings of the Orient Are, Here We Come A-Wassailing, and Little Town of Bethlehem.

Boys and girls who have originality and a gift for writing will find great pleasure in making their own shadow plays. These can be done either in prose or in verse. They can do this easily, if they keep in mind the requirements—action, dramatic interest, individuality of characters, and a simple, harmonious setting. It is worth trying.

Scenes from the cut out shadow play, "The Traveling Musicians of Bremen."

CHAPTER III

Producing Cut-out Shadow Plays

WHEN you were very young you probably were quite skilful in making shadow rabbits, ducks, and donkeys on the nursery walls. With a friend you may have cut out paper animals and people and fastened them to sticks and then made a shadow play with their shadows on the wall.

Your interest in shadows may have led you to stretch a sheet across the upper part of a doorway and cover the lower part with a shawl. Here you stood concealed from your audience while you moved your shadow figures back and forth in a lively fashion as you spoke the lines of a favorite nursery rhyme or improvised a play.

The next step was converting the old three-part screen into a shadow booth.

When one wishes to use scenery with cut-out shadows some sort of frame is necessary to hold the screen. Here is a plan for a very simple and inexpen-

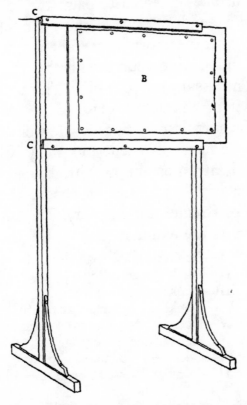

The frame (A), upon which is fastened the translucent paper or cloth (B), slides in and out of the standard at the grooves C, C.

sive standard. You can see that you can have any number of screens for this kind of standard, because it allows the screens to be slipped in and out in a moment. The materials required other than the lumber are unbleached muslin or cheap white window shades and black showcard colors, and a few brushes of different sizes. The muslin should be stretched and tacked to the frame. If you use a window shade it will not be necessary to stretch it and it provides an excellent surface on which to paint the scenery.

Making a shadow play is jolly good fun. First, make a list of the most important incidents in the story. Second, decide upon the number of scenes that you think necessary for your play. Third, decide upon the number of characters required for these scenes. You will be surprised to find how few characters and incidents are needed to tell your story. Choose only those which are most important. Know your story well before you begin. Let us choose the traveling musicians of Bremen for our play. The list of important incidents are as follows:

Incident   I—Donkey on the road
Incident   II—Donkey meets Dog
Incident   III—Donkey and Dog meet Cat
Incident   IV—Donkey, Dog, and Cat meet Cock
Incident   V—Donkey, Dog, Cat, and Cock seek shelter for night in the wood
Incident   VI—Cock sees a distant light
Incident   VII—Donkey looks through the window of the robbers' house
Incident   VIII—Donkey, Dog, Cat, and Cock break through the window
Incident   IX—Robbers flee with fright
Incident   X—The animals devour the robbers' feast
Incident   XI—The animals settle themselves for the night
Incident   XII—One of the robbers returns
Incident   XIII—He is scratched by the Cat
Incident   XIV—He is bitten by the Dog
Incident   XV—He is kicked by the Donkey
Incident   XVI—The Cock calls "Cock-a-doodle-doo"
Incident   XVII—The robber flees to his companions

Incident XVIII—The robber describes the witch that clawed him, the demon that stabbed him, the giant that beat him with a club, the fateful spirit on the roof that screamed "Throw him up to me." Four scenes will tell the story.

Scene   I—The roadside
Scene   II—The deep wood
Scene   III—The robbers' house
Scene   IV—The roadside

These four scenes require twelve characters: Donkey, Dog, Cat, Cock, Four Robbers, Witch, Demon, Giant, and the fateful spirit. Each character must be analyzed, for both disposition and general appearance.

Shadow figures require careful planning, because they present but one silhouette throughout the play. Naturally this silhouette must be the most characteristic one. The shape of the nose, chin, and head, of the hands, the feet, and the body, all must be closely studied. Let us see how a shadow figure is made. Let us begin with the Donkey. He looks old, thin, and neglected, but he still has spirit enough to start out into the world. His thin body and neck show that he is old and misused. His strong jaw shows his will and determination. Before you draw him on a piece of paper you should decide on his size. The scale is determined by the size of the shadow screen. Let us suppose that this is 21 inches by 28 inches and that your scale is two inches to the foot. The Donkey is made about $8\frac{1}{2}$ inches high by 10 inches long, the robbers 11 and 12 inches high, the Dog four inches high by 4½ inches long, and the Cock 3 inches high by 4¼ inches long. After you have drawn the Donkey to scale, cut him out and hold him behind a sheet of paper near the light and study his silhouette. Are you satisfied? If not, draw another donkey.

What is the Donkey expected to do? Move his jaw when he talks, move his tail and ears and his legs

Moving parts are pivoted with paper fasteners (a). Wires running up the sticks (f) to move the tail, neck and jaw are looped through the eyelets (c). Thumb tacks (b) or glue may be used to fasten the figure to the sticks. Pivot points should be eyeletted before inserting the fasteners; for greater ease in working, it is sometimes well to let the head of a fastener come between two parts as at (e). The movement of the jaw piece blinks the eye which is cut at (d).

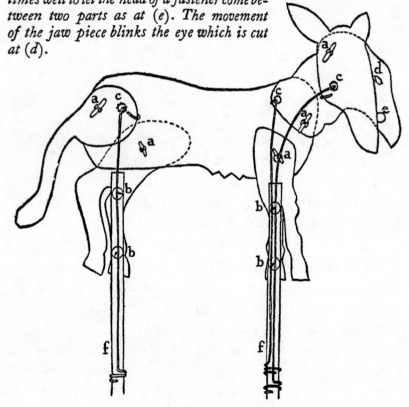

when he walks. How can this be done? The illustration may look very complicated at first. Study it carefully and follow the directions and your donkey will be able to walk, open and close his mouth, blink his eyes, and move his tail and ears. The materials that you will need are black construction paper or any heavy paper, thin sticks about 12 inches long and $\frac{3}{8}$ inch wide, eyelets, and long-pronged brass

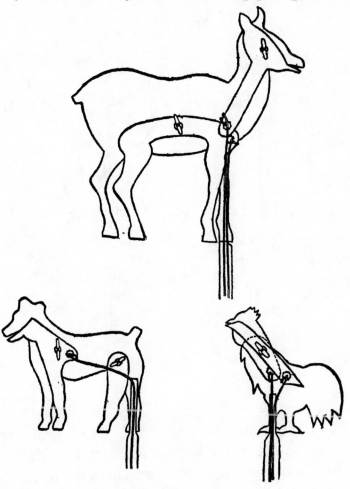

paper fasteners, thumb tacks, and light-weight wire.

Not all shadow animals are as complicated as this donkey. Here are a deer, a cock, and a dog, each made of just three pieces of paper. The illustrations

of the farmer, fairy queen, and elf (see end of chapter) will show how the human figures are made.

When you have finished constructing the cut-out

shadow figures, your next problem will be making the scenery. Composition and pattern are extremely important in shadow pictures, for nothing in the world reveals the fascination of dark and light more than the shadow play. If you can recall the beauty of the landscape in a heavy winter snowstorm when the branches and trunks of the trees are velvety black against masses of white, you can appreciate this. Every tree has a characteristic silhouette which everyone recognizes. A shadow pine tree must suggest the silhouette of the pine, likewise the oak, the elm, and the poplar, must suggest their silhouettes. So, too, with flowers and grasses. The wide prairies were suggested by the coarse prairie grass in the *Indian and the Oki*. Summer meadows were suggested by the flowers and slender grasses in *The Shepherdess*.

When you have finished the plans for a scene take crayon or soft pencil and draw it in outline on one of the screens. Use black showcard color to fill that part of your scene which is to be dark. For a black silhouette paint both sides of the screen. Distant hills and trees should be painted on one side only.

For lighting use a lantern or an extension light. Place it about six feet directly behind the screen. Color can be thrown on the screen by placing a sheet of colored gelatine in front of the light. Experiment with the light and color until you get the effects you wish.

If you use tracing cloth, such as the architects use, for your screen, you may paint on it directly, with transparent water colors. When the light comes

Behind the scenes in the human shadow play, "The Indian and the Oki." Here you can see the well-stretched sheet on its large frame, the beaver board trees (left), great rock (right), bristol board foliage, grasses, and flowers, the bridge resting on 8" horses. Notice that the actors stand very near the screen. The two actors on the right concealed by the great rock from the audience are manipulating the pair of fighting sparrows. The girl on the left is manipulating the rabbit which is shown in Scene I.

through this screen, if you have kept your colors clear, brilliant, and well related, the effect will be charming.

The shadow figure is manipulated from below. This means that you must stand below the screen so that your own shadow will not be cast upon the screen. As you bring your shadow figure forward, you will notice that as it approaches the screen it grows smaller and smaller. To prevent the figure from varying in size it should be held close against the screen.

Unlike the marionette that moves forward and backward as well as to the right and left, the shadow figure can move only to the right or left. With this limitation, however, it is surprising to find how many movements and gestures are possible. Suit the action to the word. Avoid jerky gestures and repetition of the same gesture.

The lines of the shadow play can be given by the puppeteers or by a reader or readers in front of the screen. If the puppeteers are to speak the lines they should sit down together and read the play again and again, until they can speak the lines naturally and without hesitation. When they can do this, they are ready to begin rehearsals with the shadow figures. Do not hurry. Every word should be clearly spoken.

If two or three short plays are being given in a program, two readers, one standing at the left and one at the right of the screen, can read the lines alternately.

The shadow play is a delightful kind of entertainment for young and old. It is appropriate for the home, the school, the settlement, and the Sunday school. It has the advantage of requiring very little time to produce, the materials are inexpensive, and it is an artistic means of expression.

CHAPTER IV

Producing Human Shadow Plays

DID you ever feel about your shadow as Robert Louis Stevenson did, when he wrote:

> "I have a little shadow,
>   That goes in and out with me,
> And what can be the use of him,
>   Is more than I can see."

If you ever took part in a shadow game, you discovered many surprising uses for your shadow. You may remember how you stretched a sheet in a doorway and played the game of guessing silhouettes. This was highly entertaining, and somewhat difficult when familiar faces were disguised by unusual noses and chins. Then there were the shadow charades and the game of guessing book titles.

If you wish to give a shadow play with scenery and

225

several actors performing at one time, then a large shadow screen becomes necessary. This can be made from 2-inch strips of wood, strengthened in the corners as shown in the illustration. The size of this screen will be determined by the width of the sheeting which is to cover it. The screen used at the Cleveland Museum of Art for the shadow plays *The Indian and the Oki* and *The Shepherdess* was 7¼ feet high by 12 feet long, and was covered with sheeting 90 inches in width. Great care was used in the stretching of the sheet. The tacks were placed about two inches apart.

The reason for choosing *The Indian and the Oki* for a shadow play was that it had action and characters that were very individual, such as would be easily recognized when they fell on the shadow screen. Another reason for choosing this story was that its scenery could be suggested by silhouettes. The group of boys and girls who gave this play selected important incidents of the story and re-arranged them and added incidents wherever they found it necessary. The following twelve incidents made up the first act:

1. Rabbit wiggles ears, hops across stage.

2. Sparrows scrap upon rock, first gently, growing furious.

3. Eagle swoops across and down upon rock; birds leave.

4. Wild cat moves slightly, winks eye, raises tail, arches back ready for spring as

5. Scandawatti peeps from rock, then disappears, then Indian lad appears, with bow and arrow and shoots at wild cat, hits bear.

Scenes from the human shadow play, "The Indian and the Oki"

5. Scandawatti and Achilles sit on the ground and play with their pistols.

6. Red Deer peers from behind bushes.

7. Squaw gives each boy a bowl of the stew. They eat greedily.

8. Boys undo bundle in which there are knives and beads. Achilles holds up the Oki or false face.

9. Scandawatti, alarmed, jumps up and runs. Achilles runs after him, carrying the Oki.

10. Red Deer enters, stealthily, and reaches for the pistols.

11. Achilles lifts up the Oki from behind a rock. Red Deer drops the pistols and flees.

12. Scandawatti and Achilles enter laughing, pick up weapons, wrap themselves in blankets, and lie down to sleep.

For the third act they chose the following:

1. A turkey runs across the stage.

2. Red Deer follows with Scandawatti. He binds him to a tree, then runs after the turkey.

3. Red Deer returns with dead turkey. Builds a fire and places the turkey over it.

4. Red Deer dances about, mocking Scandawatti.

5. Achilles peeks from behind rock. Motions to Scandawatti to have courage. Then sticks up the Oki and waves it about in the air.

6. Red Deer flies in terror.

7. Achilles frees Scandawatti.

8. They devour the turkey.

9. The trapper and Indian chief appear and all rejoice.

Shadow plays require just as careful character analysis as any other kind of play. Here is the character analysis.

Scandawatti, brave, loyal, fun loving.

Achilles, courageous, loyal, resourceful.

Red Deer, treacherous and superstitious.

Chief Iliol, trustworthy and dignified.

Squaw, stolid and good-natured.

Trapper, just and reliable.

Dancer, lively.

The story included the bear and turkey, the rabbit, wild cat, hawk and birds were added for the sake of the picture. The illustrations show how the turkey, wild cat, and birds were made.

The scenery consisted of tree trunks, branches, and a big rock cut from beaver board, and foliage, flowers, and grasses cut from light-weight bristol board.

The properties needed were a tripod and a kettle, a stick for the fire, a basket of corn, bowls and a ladle, pistols, strings of beads, a game bag filled with paper game, a fish basket filled with paper fish, bow and arrow, gun, rope, two blankets, and a peace pipe.

The costuming of a shadow play is quite a different problem from the costuming of any other kind of play. A costume may look quite right to the eye and yet be ineffective as a shadow. It requires ingenuity and much experimenting to produce satisfactory silhouettes. Scandawatti, Red Deer, and the dancer wore loin cloths, head band, and feathers. The Indian chief wore headdress and blanket. The squaw wore a fringed curtain, head band, and beads. The trapper

and Achilles wore trappers' costumes and coon-skin caps. A boy took the part of the bear in a bear costume made from outing flannel.

The profiles of the children were not in the least Indianlike. It was necessary to provide them with characteristic Indian noses and this was done by glueing on flat cut-out paper noses.

230

The producing of a shadow play requires a director and two assistants, as well as the group of actors. The director is responsible for the production of the play which will probably require five or six rehearsals. During the first rehearsal he stays behind the screen, working out with the group each incident of the play. He and the group decide upon the entrances, positions on the bridge, the exits, and those who are to manipulate the shadow animals receive their instructions. The reader should be present at the first rehearsal, in order to observe the development of the play. At this rehearsal the actors need not be in costume. Each actor begins by interpreting his part as he feels it should be done. The Director should inspire and encourage his actors to do their best and guard against being too critical at this time, since everyone is feeling his way—becoming familiar with properties, and with this new kind of acting in one plane.

It was in the first rehearsal of the *Indian and the Oki* that the boy who took the part of Scandawatti discovered, as he was trying to escape from the bear, that it would look more natural if he got out of the bear's reach by climbing the rock, rather than by dodging behind it. When a stepladder was placed behind the beaver-board rock, the boy, after much practice, was able to make it appear to the audience that he was really climbing the rock. He was finally able to give a little slip as he reached the top, just as the bear was about to overtake him. This gave a real thrill to the young spectators.

At the second rehearsal the Director takes his position in front of the screen. He watches every movement and gesture of the actors. He guides the actors who cannot see their shadows, because they are so close to the screen. If he understands pattern and rhythm he can direct their movements so that every movement of the shadow play will be beautiful. The reader begins his part at the second rehearsal. He can give an introduction and carry the story on between the acts, or he can read as the play is being given. The reader may be a girl or a boy and should be chosen for a rich, well-modulated voice, dramatic sense, and ability to enunciate distinctly. The reader should be appropriately costumed.

Introducing a dancer in a shadow play presents a problem. In the second scene of *The Indian and the Oki* you can see in the illustration how the height, and bulk, and dignity of the Indian chief on the left and the curved line of the trapper's body on the right were used to frame the space for the rhythmic movements of the dancer. The dancer also had his problems. The first was that of keeping a characteristic Indian silhouette on the screen at all times. The second problem was that of varying his movements to show his veneration for his chief and his adoration for the Great Spirit. The beating of the tomtom gave the tempo for the steps of his dance. A teacher who understood folk dancing coached the boy who took this part outside of the regular rehearsals, so that he might gain confidence and skill.

By the fourth or fifth rehearsal, if the actors can interpret their part naturally and convincingly, they

More scenes from the human shadow play,
"The Indian and the Oki."

will be ready to put on their costumes. Here many surprises await them. As an illustration of this the shepherdess in the play by that name made, for herself, a very correct little bodice. When she appeared on the shadow screen her silhouette was very disappointing. In order to give the right effect, a short length of cheesecloth was slashed six or seven times at the ends, and then drawn tightly around her, and the slashed ends were tied together down the front. You can see her in the illustration, as she kneels on the bridge manipulating one of the fighting sparrows in the first scene of *The Indian and the Oki*. The long heavy braids of this shepherdess were made of yarn.

Any ordinary lantern or an electric light with a reflector may be used for lighting the screen. A screen 7 by 12 feet will require a 400-watt light placed about eighteen feet behind it. If you have very little space behind your screen, your lantern may throw a large disk of light. You can avoid this disk by fastening to the front of the lantern a piece of asbestos with an opening cut to the same proportions as the screen.

There are many possibilities of using color in a shadow play. A safe rule to follow is either to use color throughout a play or not to use color at all. A sheet of colored gelatine placed in front of the light will diffuse color over the entire screen. The time of day can be suggested by color: pink for early morning, yellow for noon, yellow-orange for the late afternoon, blue or blue-green for night.

In the second scene of *The Indian and the Oki*,

yellow-orange gelatine was used to indicate the late summer afternoon. Under the cardboard kettle a red bulb, partly concealed by sticks and twigs, suggested fire.

The depths of the sea can be suggested by covering the light with green gelatine and using cut-out shells, seaweeds, and water plants as scenery. Water sprites and fanciful sea creatures would be at home in such a setting.

Music is a beautiful accompaniment for shadow plays, especially for Christmas and Easter celebrations. Imagine a shadow play in six scenes built about the Nativity according to the gospels of St. Matthew and St. Luke.

Scene I—The Annunciation

"The angel Gabriel was sent from God unto a city of Galilee, named Nazareth, to a virgin espoused to a man whose name was Joseph, of the house of David; and the virgin's name was Mary. And the angel came in unto her, and said, 'Hail, thou that art highly favored, the Lord is with thee; blessed art thou among women.'" (St. Luke, I: 26, 27, 28.)

Scene II—The Angel and the Shepherds

"And there were in the same country, shepherds abiding in the field, keeping watch over their flocks by night. And, lo, the angel of the Lord came upon them, and the glory of the Lord shone round about them: and they were sore afraid. And the angel said unto them, 'Fear not, for behold, I bring you good

234

tidings of great joy, which shall be to all people. For unto you is born this day in the city of David, a Saviour, which is Christ the Lord. And this shall be a sign unto you; Ye shall find the babe wrapped in swaddling clothes, lying in a manger.' And suddenly there was with the angel a multitude of the heavenly host praising God, and saying, 'Glory to God in the highest, and on earth, peace and good will toward men.' And it came to pass, as the angels were gone away from them into heaven, the shepherds said to one another, 'Let us now go even unto Bethlehem, and see this thing which is come to pass, which the Lord hath made known unto us.'" (St. Luke, II: 3–16.)

Scene III—The Adoration of the Shepherds

"The Shepherds came with haste, and found Mary, and Joseph, and the babe lying in a manger." (St. Luke, II: 17.)

Scene IV—The Coming of the Wise Men

"Now when Jesus was born in Bethlehem of Judea in the days of Herod the king, behold, there came wise men from the east to Jerusalem, saying, 'Where is he that is born King of the Jews? For we have seen his star in the east and are come to worship him.'" (St. Matthew, II: 1, 3.)

Scene V—Simeon and the Young Child

"And behold there was a man in Jerusalem, whose name was Simeon; and the same man was just and devout, waiting for the consolation of Israel: and the

Holy Ghost was upon him, and it was revealed unto him by the Holy Ghost that he should not see death before he had seen the Lord's Christ. And he came by Spirit into the Temple: and when the parents brought the Child Jesus, to do for him after the custom of the law, then took he him up in his arms, and blessed God, and said, 'Lord, now lettest thou thy servant depart in peace, according to thy word: for mine eyes have seen thy salvation, which thou hast prepared before the face of all peoples: a light to lighten the Gentiles and the glory of thy people Israel.'" (St. Luke, II: 25, 33.)

Scene VI—The Flight into Egypt

"And the angel of the Lord appeared to Joseph in a dream, saying, 'Arise, and take the young Child and his mother, and flee into Egypt, and be thou there until I bring thee word: for Herod will seek the young Child to destroy him.' When he arose he took the young Child and his mother by night, and departed into Egypt, and was there until the death of Herod; that it might be fulfilled which was spoken of the Lord by the prophet, saying, 'Out of Egypt have I called my son.'" (St. Matthew, II: 13, 11.)

These incidents, so simple, vivid, and beautiful when reverently interpreted as shadow plays, seem to carry something of the age-old mystery of the shadow.

In the East, shadow plays are an intimate part of the everyday life of the people. In the Western world

Scenes from the human shadow play, "The Shepherdess."

they have, so far, meant very little. European artists have already discovered their possibilities and are even carrying the shadow into the world of the movie, revealing new fields as a challenge to our creative efforts.

BIBLIOGRAPHY

BIBLIOGRAPHY

A List of Books Suggested for the Making of Marionette Plays

,

A LIST OF BOOKS SUGGESTED
FOR THE MAKING OF
MARIONETTE PLAYS

,

HUMOROUS TALES

Alice's Adventures in Wonderland, by Carroll. Macmillan

Gulliver's Travels, by Swift. Macmillan

Don Quixote, by Cervantes. Dodd

Peter and Wendy, by Barrie. Scribner

Just So Stories, by Kipling. Doubleday

Uncle Remus, by Harris. Appleton

Tom Sawyer, by Clemens. Harper

Alice, Through the Looking Glass, by Carroll. Macmillan

Pinocchio, the Story of a Marionette, by Lorenzini. Ginn

Midsummer Night's Dream, by Shakespeare. Edited by Rolfe, Am. Book Co., Hudson, Ginn

Rip Van Winkle, by Irving. Macmillan

Arabian Nights, by Colum. Macmillan

Rose and the Ring, by Thackeray, Stokes. Macmillan

Wind in the Willows, by Grahame. Scribner

Tales of Laughter, by Wiggin and Smith. Doubleday

TALES OF ADVENTURE

The Boy's Percy, by Lanier. Scribner
The Black Arrow, By Stevenson. Scribner
William Tell, by Schmidt & Marshall. McClurg,
    Dutton
Treasure Island, by Stevenson, Scribner
Men of Iron, by Pyle. Harper
Wonder Book by Hawthorne. Houghton
Otto of the Silver Hand, by Pyle. Scribner
The Boy's Froissart, Ed. by Lanier. Scribner
Tales from the Alhambra, by Irving. Houghton
Story of the Canterbury Pilgrims, retold by Darton,
    by Chaucer. Stokes
The Lance of Kanana, by French. Lathrop
With Spurs of Gold, by Greene. Little
The Golden Perch, by Hutchinson. Longmans
Captains Courageous, by Kipling. Doubleday
The Book of Bravery, by Lanier. Scribner
The Last of the Mohicans, by Cooper. Holt

'

UNCLASSIFIED

Little Women, by Alcott. Little
Bird's Christmas Carol, by Wiggin. Houghton
Rip Van Winkle, by Irving. Macmillan
Oliver Twist, by Dickens. Scribner
Prince and the Pauper, by Clemens. Macmillan
The Christmas Carol, by Dickens. Macmillan
Heidi, by Spyri. Ginn. Houghton
Cricket on the Hearth, by Dickens. Rand
David Copperfield, by Dickens. Scribner
The Tempest, by Shakespeare, Ed. Rolfe. Amer. Bk.
    Co., Hudson, Ginn
The Merchant of Venice, by Shakespeare, Ed. Rolfe.
    Amer. Bk. Co., Hudson, Ginn
The King of the Golden River, by Ruskin. Page
Master Skylark, by Bennett. Century
Gabriel and His Hour Book, by Stein. Page
The Piper, by Peabody. Houghton
Evangeline, by Longfellow. Houghton
Story Telling Ballads, by Olcott. Houghton
Hiawatha, by Longfellow. Houghton
Lady of the Lake, by Scott. Houghton
Lays of Ancient Rome, by Macauley. Houghton
The Pied Piper of Hamlin, by Browning. Rand

A SHORT LIST OF
REFERENCE BOOKS
ON COSTUME

,

A SHORT LIST OF REFERENCE BOOKS ON COSTUME

The Heritage of Dress, by Webb. London, E. Grant Richards

A Study of Costume, by Sage. Scribner

Chats on Costume, by Rhead. Stokes

Dress Design, by Hughes. Macmillan

Greek Dress, by Abrahams. London, John Murray

British Costume During 19 Centuries, by Ashdown. Edinburgh, T. C. & E. C. Jack

The History of Fashion in France, Tr. by Mrs. Hoey & M. Lillie. London, Scribner and Wetford

Costuming a Play, by Elizabeth Grimball & Rhea Wells. Century

Historic Dress in America, by McClellan. Jacobs

The Encyclopædia Britannica

A SHORT LIST OF BOOKS
ON MARIONETTES

A SHORT LIST OF BOOKS ON MARIONETTES

Heroes of the Puppet Stage, by Anderson. Harcourt
The Book of Marionettes, by Joseph. Huebsch
The Tony Sarg Marionette Book, McIsaacs. Greenburg
The Mask—Vols. I—VIII, by Craig
The Marionette, by Craig

There are also many excellent books on the subject
of Marionettes in French, German, and Italian.
These are very exhaustive studies, fully illustrated, that will repay investigation.

,

A SHORT LIST OF BOOKS THAT
CONTAIN INFORMATION
ON THE
MASK AND SHADOWS

,

THE MASK

Masks and Demons, by Macgowan & Rosse. Harcourt
The Golden Bough, by Frazer. Macmillan
History of the Harlequinade, by Sand. Lippincott
Clowns, by Disher. Constable
Manners, Customs & Dress of the Middle Ages, by
    LaCroix. Appleton
The Theater of the Greek, by Donaldson. Macmillan
The Greek Theater, by Flickinger. University of
    Chicago
History of Classical Greek Literature, by Mahaffy.
    Macmillan
Noh, by Fenelossa & Pound. Knopf
Field Museum Guide—Part I, by Laufer. Field
    Museum
The NO Plays of Old Japan, by Stopes. Dutton
The NO Plays of Japan, by Waley. Knopf
Medicine-Men of the Apache, by Bourke
9th Annual Report, U. S. Bureau of American Ethnology
Tusayan Katcinas, by Fewkes
*15th Annual Report, U. S. Bureau of American
    Ethnology*
The Point Barrow Eskimo, by Murdoch
6th Annual Report, U. S. Bureau of American Ethnology

There are several excellent books on Masks in French,
    German, and Italian

SHADOWS

The Golden Bough, by Frazer, Macmillan
Field Museum Guide, by Laufer. Field Museum
The Book of Marionettes, by Joseph Huebsch Viking
  Press
A Book about the Theater, by Mathews. Viking Press
Masks and Demons, by Macgowan and Rosse.
  Harcourt

Very important work in this field has been done by
  the German writers, Georg Jacob, Otto Höver,
  Wilhelm Grube, and Hellmut Ritter.

INDEX

INDEX

Index

Index

Index

LaVergne, TN USA
16 May 2010
182839LV00002B/1/A